BECOME A MASTER OF PERSUASION
2-in-1 Bundle

How to Influence People

+

5 Hours of Positive Affirmations –

The #1 Beginner's Box Set to Advanced Manipulation Techniques and Boost Your Confidence

HOW TO INFLUENCE PEOPLE AND BECOME A MASTER OF PERSUASION

Discover Advanced Methods to Analyze People, Control Emotions and Body Language. Leverage Manipulation in Business & Relationships

By John Clark

TABLE OF CONTENTS

Introduction 7
Chapter 1 Manipulation as a tool of masters 8
    The secrets of the greatest men 9
    The often overlooked human need to be manipulated 11
    Manipulation is not evil, it's just a tool 13
Chapter 2 Mastering your emotions and reactions 15
    Know YOURSELF (tHIS IS KEY) 15
    Be the master of your emotions 17
    Develop your instincts 19
Chapter 3 Knowledge of emotional reactions and how to read them 21
    Knowing your mark 22
    Observing and translating emotional reactions 23
    Learn to take a clue 24
    To react or to obey: The key to always getting it right 25
    Practice makes perfect 25
Chapter 4 Understanding basic body language 27
    Understanding from less than words 28
    The little things are usually most important 32
    Recognizing tells and signs could be an art or science 32
    Recognizing a target 33
    Warning signs 35
Chapter 5 Persuasion: the psychological theories 37
    The psychological perspective 41
Chapter 6 Persuasion: The practical 44
    Putting the theories into practice 44
    Other techniques of persuasion 48
    Reverse psychology 51
    Remember to always analyze before making your move 52

Chapter 7 Common manipulation techniques 53
    Manipulation is not always for the faint hearted 63
Chapter 8 Mastering the art of subtlety-DO NOT BE
BLATANT 64
    The cautious approach is always best 65
    A flimsy ploy is ineffective 65
    Never get ahead of yourself 66
    Never go all out unless.. 67
Chapter 9 Practical uses of manipulation 68
    Manipulation in business 68
    Manipulation in relationships 70
    Manipulating a friend 71
    Seductive manipulation 72
    How to properly manipulate strangers 72
Chapter 10 Manipulating and Scouting: The Forgotten
Connection 74
    Watching your target is important 75
    Establishing trust 76
    Planning a strategy of approach 76
    Follow only what you see or hear 77
Conclusion.. 79

Congratulations on purchasing "How to Influence People and Become A Master of Persuasion" and thank you for doing so!

The following chapters will discuss about the power of Persuasion, learn how to Control Your Emotions, read body language to analyse people and many more Manipulation tactics you will be able to use in Business, Relationships, and with Friends. The information found in this book will best explore the techniques you need to learn so you will be able to master The Psychology of Persuasion

Thanks again for choosing this book! Every effort was made to ensure it is full of as much useful information as possible. Please enjoy!

INTRODUCTION

There is a belief amongst most people that when sequences and situations are created to change the perception and reactions of a person, it is a negative thing. But if we were to look closely, we would observe that this is something that manifests on a daily basis in our lives. we are constantly trying to change how people see us and the things we do. Sometimes we want them to view us in a positive way and other times in a negative way, depending on what we want to achieve at that moment in time. Some people call this manipulation and it is indeed so but manipulation is not necessarily evil as most people would lead you to believe. Many believe it to be associated with only exploitation and deception for personal gain but fail to praise such tactics when they are used positively in eliminating unhealthy habits and behaviors.

To put this in perspective, do you remember the days when your parents had to promise you gifts and extra play time just to get you to complete your homework? That is manipulation in its simplest form but it doesn't match up with what people like to believe of manipulation. They clearly were not manipulating your reasoning for their own benefit, if anything, it was for yours.

People turn to manipulation for a variety of reasons; to advance their own purposes and agendas, to help you attain your own goals and objectives, to gain power or simply because they find it interesting. The last of these reasons is usually the most dangerous because such people are usually oblivious to the damage they can cause or are already causing until they are too far gone in the game. Such people keep manipulating everyone every time without the slightest hint of guilt. Such people are psychopaths.

This book is has not been produced to turn anyone into a psychopath nor is it written to challenge the status quo of manipulation in the world. It is written to show you the ropes at a skill many already utilize. Yes, everyday people manipulate others; in their business environments, in social settings, in friendships and relationships. So, it is high time you sat down and learnt the tricks to an art that all influential people possess.

CHAPTER 1

MANIPULATION AS A TOOL OF MASTERS

In the world nowadays, a variety of situations necessitates or determines ascribing someone the title of master. But in all of those situations, the master is the one who has most influence on the people around him or her. The power such a master possesses could have initially been attained by skill or reputation but to avoid losing it over time, the master has to be adept at retaining his or her influence. Such a person is usually held in high regard, regardless of status or wealth and vary rarely do these people attain such a status by being themselves or by being ordinary. Being so might make people to like and admire you but true respect and power over others must be gotten by other means. This is where manipulation comes in.

Manipulation goes hand in hand with power. Wherever you can sense the effect of manipulation, there is bound to be an imbalance of power. The power in such societies is usually concentrated in the hands of a few who could be referred to as masters over others. These people are well versed at making people think along the same lines as them, making people act along the same lines as them, making people follow them unconditionally and generally being able to influence the thoughts and opinions of those around them effectively.

If you were to look back in history at some of the most influential people, one of the things you would observe is that the ideas they advocated were not necessarily moral or even right at all. Their beliefs were not necessarily righteous or ethical, but whenever they needed it, people and followers flocked to their sides, ready to follow them to the end and ready to defend the ideas they had been taught to believe and defend. From terrorist leaders to controversial politicians and men of power who regardless of the revulsion their ideas seemed to generate still seemed to be gaining more power. Why was this so? Because they knew how to influence and control people. It didn't matter what they said but provided they could make people think how they wanted them to and act how they wanted them to, they were never at risk of being powerless. Their power didn't originate from a sense of righteousness or correctness but from the sense of followership they were able to instill in people.

It is this sense of followership and loyalty that you should aim to achieve through manipulation. Manipulation is not just your key to power, it is your key to success because with power comes the ability to thrive off people in any environment. This ability is inherent in all successful people. Whether you are an entrepreneur or someone with a daily job, as long as people are involved, the knowledge of people and how to influence them is necessary for your success.

Some people have those once in a lifetime ideas or a revolutionary approach to solving a problem but without the knowledge of how to thrive on the backs of others, they would never be able to fully consolidate on what they have. The ability to manipulate people is yours to use as you wish; you could use it in your search for personal happiness or in your quest for wealth and affluence, whichever one is your choice. This book, however, has only one aim; helping you become a master in whatever you chose to be or do.

THE SECRETS OF THE GREATEST MEN

Manipulation and deception are one of the numerous skills possessed by the greatest and most powerful men to have roamed this earth. Not all men are Gandhi and if the history books were properly scoured and its annals scrutinized, many of the men who have exerted the most influence on the world would be shown to be manipulators who merely hid their more negatively perceived talents in a shroud of piety, idealism and oratory.

This is not to say that these men were evil or bad, they just understood the need to do what was necessary when necessary and if this involved tweaking the emotions and thoughts of people to generate reactions that were favorable to their causes, so be it.

And so, the truth behind many of the world's greatest men and leaders is not divine intervention or an alignment of the stars but rather a lack of the emotional restrictions that plague the ordinary man. Many of these men from Caesar to Napoleon weren't evil or psychopathic but had a goal and a vision of the world that couldn't be achieved by simply following the rules and hoping that every other person saw things the same way they did. No, great men do not wait, they act.

Not to limit this to only men, we have had some pretty powerful women in the past who understood that to wield real power was not a matter of honesty or being a good wife but rather how to get people to do what you want when you want it. That is the essence of manipulation, to get people so dependent and so in awe of you that you could easily influence their principles and guide their actions in the direction you believe it ought to be going in. Take for instance, the sexual manipulation of both Caesar and Mark Anthony by Cleopatra in a bid to protect her interests and titles. It is mostly overlooked but that has in no way detracted from her brilliant manipulation of two very powerful men.

What I am trying to say here is that many of the events that have shaped the world politically, industrially, even religiously are so mired in manipulation, it's hard to dismiss its usefulness in both the old days and the modern world. It is used as a business tactic, as a means of motivation or as an aid to persuasion in almost any facet of life.

In the modern world, manipulation is synonymous with politics and is widely thought to be used only by politicians, business executives and the likes but if you look closely, you would see that we all practice a form of manipulation. In fact, any setting in which there seems to be an imbalance of power probably contains an element of manipulation and since this imbalance in power is a staple of the realistic world, it could be said that manipulation is rife in the world and in our everyday life. There is manipulation in our daily interactions, in our personal relationships, our business relationships and even religious interactions. Consider the clergy who spends a large chunk of his sermon emphasizing on punishment of sin and the travails of hell, he might be speaking the truth but his words are meant to impart fear in you and it is that fear which he counts on to make the difference in your approach to life. That is a classic case of emotional manipulation using fear. The cleric does not mean to do this but deep down he realizes that this is the most effective way of knocking into people the need for his or her God. He does not mean to manipulate you but he does it nonetheless. That is what manipulation is. You might truly respect the autonomy of a person but when you feel you need to influence them, you could unknowingly find yourself trying to take advantage of their emotions and this means you are manipulating them. You do not have to be evil, you simply need to recognize the necessity for a line of action and possess the strength of mind to do what needs to be done.

Over the course of this audio book, you would learn how to wield similar power over people, how to make yourself indispensable and how to make yourself capable of greatness.

THE OFTEN OVERLOOKED HUMAN NEED TO BE MANIPULATED

As humans we have all been blessed with autonomy, the right to make our own decisions and live by them and any threat to such autonomy generally has us on guard. That is the reason why when faced with anything, law or person we believe aims to rip this independence from us, we fight back with or without violence. Take into consideration the numerous uprisings in history as proof of this. The people who led the French and English revolutions did not possess more power than the monarchs in power but when they felt their needs being thrown out the door and their independence being preyed upon, they fought back and they fought hard.

Our history when it comes to defending our independence is quite rich, from the early advocates of our modern religions facing up to the idol worshippers in their day to the women throughout history who have fought for equal rights. They might not have realized what they were doing but they were exercising an innate human need to be free. But just as the need to be free exists, so does the need to be controlled or the need for order.

This need to be controlled is the reason why humans needed monarchs and governments to rule and govern their daily life. Because if left to live life freely and unchecked, we would have been consumed by chaos. But as our population grew and we expanded to cover more territory, so did the influence of such monarchs and governments, the controlling forces, on our life wear thin, eventually becoming insignificant. Though this is on a much grander scale and might, it is a larger manifestation of our need to sometimes be guided by others. Thus, it is apt to say that every one of us needs guidance.

The guidance might be spiritual, academic or psychological but if we were to trace the source of our knowledge, we would find that it must have originated from a person or book and very rarely is it completely original. To better understand this, consider how you always feel the need to try and impart the knowledge you have unto others either by holding lectures or by giving advice. This need to guide one another is how we humans have passed our knowledge over millenniums.

It is because of this inherent need for guidance, knowledge and control that we are susceptible to manipulation. I am not saying that anybody deserves to be manipulated but that everybody can be manipulated. And since whatever is possible is always done, the possibility of being manipulated means that some of us, or rather, many of us are bound to fall victim to people whose goal is to manipulate us. It is the way of the world, the only difference between you and the next person is how good you are at it and how you want to use your influence and skill.

MANIPULATION IS NOT EVIL, IT'S JUST A TOOL

It is widely believed that manipulation is evil, I neither support nor assent to this belief. Manipulation is the use of any sort of influence, be it physical, emotional or financial, over a person, group or situation to generate a desired outcome. The outcome is most likely one which favors you and your goals but does not necessarily need to be detrimental to other people involved. On another note, the belief of manipulation being negative usually assumes that this goal you want to achieve is not in sync with that of your mark or target. But, what if it does? Won't it then be more apt to classify your manipulation as a means of motivation or, at the very least, as a positive influence? Consider this:

You have a boss who is hell bent on following a particular line of action as regards a new business deal yet facts and your gut tell you that his approach or decision is a wrong one. But he refuses to listen to the opinions of anyone, probably because his stance is as a result of a very old sentiment or bias. In this case, every straightforward and honest approach has failed. Wouldn't it be better to manipulate and tweak his emotions just a little bit and save his job and the company's balance sheet from recording a loss?

In such a case, your manipulation of your boss is still considered immoral but on the general balance of events, it is the right course of action if all means of rational persuasion have been exhausted. From a conventional point of view, the idea of one person manipulating another is considered a criticism of the manipulator's behavior, but is manipulation always immoral? The above example doesn't seem immoral. When looked at on a grander scale, we would most likely agree that manipulation is rife in our everyday life but the only times it is actually classified as evil or bad is when it leads to harm, be it emotional or psychological, of the target. Sure, manipulation can expose vulnerabilities that otherwise might have remained hidden. Yes, manipulation could lead to oppression of people but it could also be the only way to achieve a truly noble goal. Consider this next example.

Assuming you are a security officer who was unlucky enough to be on duty on the day a terrorist was captured and you have credible intel that the terrorist is slated to carry out an attack on that very day or maybe during the week. You have tried every possible method of rational reasoning from trying to tap into his or her empathy to offering deals but the terrorist has refused to budge and the only way to extract the information without resorting to violence is to employ manipulation as a tool. Is this considered immoral or is the immorality simply justified simply because you get to save many lives?

Depending on your answer to the above question, the knowledge shared in this book might one day be beneficial to you. If you possess a hardline view on the perception of manipulation and are of the opinion that it can never be used for a positive goal, the knowledge of this book is of no practical use to you and you are better served stopping here and picking a book that is more acceptable and is less likely to offend your sensibilities.

CHAPTER 2

MASTERING YOUR EMOTIONS AND REACTIONS

Manipulation is a game of emotions, knowing how to read them, how to tweak them, how to play them, erase them, create them and react to them. Every manipulative move should be aimed at exposing the emotional core of your mark or target because that is the only way to owning their actions and decisions. But for you to adequately and efficiently effect your desired change in the individual or group of relevance, you have to have an understanding of yourself and your emotions. To put it cleanly, you have to know yourself more than any other person because only then can you make a move at controlling others.

KNOW YOURSELF (THIS IS KEY)

Knowing yourself is key if not the most important ingredient to possess before you embark on the road to mastering people. This is because, to avoid overreaching or underestimating yourself, you have to possess an understanding of your abilities, a keen sense as to where your strengths end and where your weaknesses begin. Only with this knowledge can you decipher the direction in which you should be leading your mark and the approach you should be taking to do so.

Such in depth knowledge of oneself would require a level of truthfulness in accepting one's limitations and a further level of self-discipline to avoid crossing those limits. The idea behind getting under your target's defenses would vary depending on the target but would require you to either play up your weaknesses while emphasizing your strengths or play up your strengths while emphasizing your weaknesses. Both require you to be alert.

As important as understanding your limits is, it would be nothing without an understanding of your emotions and that would be incomplete without the ability to recognize your emotional markers. These markers are what people see regardless of what goes on in your head and thus, are more likely to influence their thoughts. This knowledge is not achieved by simply making a resolution but by logically analyzing your every move in a bid to pinpoint how your internal emotions manifest as external actions. This might seem complex but it is actually quite easy. It just involves thinking about your reactions and emotion as two separate entities then following them through step by step to the end and figuring out how one influences the other. Let me give you a hypothetical situation.

A friend of yours who is usually quiet and reserved walks up to you one day and shoves you in the back in a moment of excitement. It was a playful shove but you not realizing it were this particular friend turns back and are about to express your anger before you notice him and check yourself. He sees this and wonders why you would react in such a way and in a playful manner shoves you again. This time however, you don't check yourself but instead launch into a tirade.

At the time he hit you the first time, let's assume you were in a rather normal state, not particularly angry or happy. After the first hit, you got angry but controlled yourself. While this control is necessary to possess for the skill you are learning, the important part of your analysis should be what gave your anger away since you had not actually reacted. You have to know if it was a clenched fist by your side, a hardened facial expression, a twitching eye or whatever because controlling the reaction is only half the lesson, you have to behave outwardly like the thought of a reaction never even crossed your mind. This is the kind of logical breakdown you must grow adept at performing on yourself and your actions. You must abandon the ordinary man's habits of reacting impulsively and start reacting logically. Next, you have to consider your loss of control on the succeeding incident. Such a reaction could point to the shove itself being an act that ticks you off, an underlying problem or problems with the aforementioned friend or even your limit in such situations.

Whichever one it is, you need to get a handle on it and eliminate all emotions from your reactions unless when you feel it has to be released.

BE THE MASTER OF YOUR EMOTIONS

Other than your strengths and weaknesses, another key area of your life and being to pay attention to is your emotions. Most people underestimate the need for a control over their emotions and that is the major reason they have little control over the emotions of others. I am not advising for you to remain meek regardless of the provocation or for you to flare up at the slightest sign of resistance. No, what I am saying is that you have to be able to control whatever reaction is necessary in the moment, to bring it out at a moment's notice and to lock it back up when it has served its purpose. You need to recognize your emotional triggers and work at dulling their effect. Failing at such an important facet of your person could lead you to unwillingly push a target too far or to allow a target run wild and free for too long. Meanwhile, mastering the control of your emotion in this way would give the double advantage of reducing the ability people possess to rile you up or manipulate you while also granting you complete autonomy over your own reactions.

As I implied earlier, different targets require different approaches and different treatments and for this reason different emotions would elicit different effects on them. Where anger might cause one to be subservient, it might cause another to be more belligerent. This is the major reason you have to master not just the ability to act and create emotional reactions but also the ability to suppress your more natural emotional reactions as these said reactions can interfere with the image you are trying to portray.

Your control on your emotions is one of the major tools by which you control the perception people have of you and when it comes to manipulating people, it is key that you control their perception of you because only then would you control how they will treat you. It is important for you to remember that the initial way by which people judge another's character is through his or her behavior and emotional disposition and as such, control over both would grant onto you the power to control people's perception of you.

From another angle, your emotional disposition towards issues and events is usually a cornerstone of your reputation, at least in the minds of most people. This is a weakness in people. They assume that emotions are almost unchangeable thereby nullifying the possibility in their minds that one is capable of manipulating his or her emotions to deceive them. They believe that your reaction to a situation would always stay constant unless another effect is in play. The trick is introducing another reaction/emotion that contradicts your normal in a bid to gain their attention while lowering their defenses to deal with your perceived soft spot.

Because of this nullification, this is a belief you must always be out to take advantage of. The warning behind this is that before attempting to cash in on this mistake, you have to have fine-tuned your ability to act out scenarios and create emotions. If you are not well versed at this, a smart target might figure out your play before you are even started.

Furthermore, when utilizing this weakness, the emotion being introduced should be as evanescent as possible so as not to confuse the target. What I mean is that, with such a tactic, the effect you are going for is the **"oh, that is so unlike him"** effect and not the **"oh, he has changed so much from the time we met"** effect. This means that the emotion to be introduced should be temporary and fleeting, only surfacing for a brief period of time. Most times, the tactic is effective for a particular emotion only once or twice and should never be attempted consecutively using the same emotion. Here is an illustration of this particular trick.

The target is a female and you have gone through the basics with her, establishing a character and manufacturing reactions for every predictable action of hers. In your bid to seduce her, you have gotten to first base, first kiss and now you are looking to score a big finish and leave. But she's been very coy and defensive about sex and you haven't been able to lower her defenses on the issue. One day an issue comes up between you guys and ordinarily you would have let it slide with a smile but instead you flare up for a bit and take to keeping to yourself. She avoids bringing up the issue for a while but later comes in for the conversation.

The major point here is the change from your regular emotional reaction to a more aggressive one. This would prompt her to believe that you might have lost a little bit of emotional control and seeing as such instability is a constant source of discussion in relationships, your current countenance would require her to have a conversation with you. Bear in mind that the conversation is not for you to petulantly complain about her not having sex with you but rather for you to make her feel she is in a position of power to broker peace while considering you to be the victim. You are not to make things overly hard or easy for her. Your time to act would come after you have settled the quarrel. It would be right for you to initiate a make out session rather than ask her to have sex. This moment in which she has lowered her defenses to accommodate your emotional issues is when you make your move and if you have played your cards right up to that moment, you are about to get that score you have been hoping for. From then onwards, it is up to you to proceed as you wish but with smarts of course. Do not forget, overusing this tactic increases the possibility of exposing your game to your target.

DEVELOP YOUR INSTINCTS

Instincts are natural; they are either borne from experience or you are born with them. It is that voice in your head that speaks to you when you are in a fix and need a quick solution to your problem. It is the one that guides most of your impulsive reactions. I bet you used to doubt your impulses could change but trust me they can. Many people believe impulses can only be controlled but that is for someone who still wants to possess impulses. Real masters of emotions do not just control their impulses, they eliminate them. Only when those impulses are absent do the instincts you have trained yourself in start to kick in.

Our instincts are a product of our deeper nature, our deeper understanding and our environment. They usually mirror the things we have learnt and experienced. When we act on our instincts, were basically surrendering to our past experiences and innermost directions. These directions can be changed but not easily. To truly develop your instincts is not a matter of turning pages or staring at a screen and absorbing words but rather putting your skills to the test in real life and facing failure because only with these can you correct the folly of past experiences and create new directions. You have to put your newly learned tactics to work, feel them out, recognize how to make them click for you and depending on what you succeed or fail at, your mind will automatically store all of these experiences as either positive results inducing actions or negative results inducing actions. It is based on the presence of this more advanced knowledge that your instincts become sharper and more trustworthy because you stop making decisions steeped in theoretical propaganda and start making experienced decisions.

Instincts are necessary in understanding people and situations because only when you know what to look out for can you correctly react but in instances when the mark is still more of a stranger, you have to rely on your instincts and experiences to guess what type of person you are dealing with in terms of temperament, likes, dislikes, potential tells and the likes. Without the necessary sharp instincts, these would be quite difficult if not impossible.

CHAPTER 3

KNOWLEDGE OF EMOTIONAL REACTIONS AND HOW TO READ THEM

Reading people is arguably the most vital tool to a successful manipulation. This might be an art to some or a science to others depending on if they are naturally talented at it or if it is a completely acquired skill. Don't get me wrong, I do not mean to say that some are born with the ability to read people. What I mean is that it comes easier to some people with time than others.

Reading people and their emotions is a historically difficult task and yet without it, attempting a manipulation is akin to a blind man climbing a mountain. Many believe it to be about making snap decisions based on how people look and jumping to conclusions before you have even shared a word but in truth, it is way more than that. Before we jump into this, I should warn you that psychologists have confirmed that there is no foolproof way to read or decipher people and I would like to personally add that many of the methods you might learn might seem contradictory. Having said this, it is up to you to engage your wits and let your instincts guide you.

A key facet of reading people is their emotional disposition towards various situations. To really understand them through this means, you need to have watched them react to a few situations so as to give you a feel as to how they might react in similar and contrasting settings. However, emotions are notoriously difficult to decipher and many amateurs make the mistake of translating signs and gestures into singular meanings. This is wrong because a sign could denote multiple possible emotions.

It is due to this possibility that signs and gestures should not be treated or read as individual entities but rather should be taken contextually, while also putting into consideration other facts available to you. The last ingredient that is needed to make the result of a reading as close to reality as possible is a sharp instinct. I have spoken about developing this in chapter 2 and will refrain from discussing further but in my opinion, it is the most important tool for reading people.

KNOWING YOUR MARK

The first step to reading a mark or target is to abandon all of your previous projections and prejudices about people. These prejudices could be racial, ethnic etc. but they should all be thrown out because without a clean slate on which to present your facts, you risk destroying your readings with bias and sentiments. As a manipulator, your main goal in reading people, especially strangers, is not to spot deceit but to spot openings which could be used to forge connections or to discover character traits that could be used to your advantage. I would advise that when initially attempting manipulations, you pick targets that are more insecure, lonely or are possessing of low self-esteem. This is usually obvious from their need to defend themselves regularly, an eagerness to join or participate in a conversation, shyness, tendency to back down from confrontations and similar behaviors.

A general way to get people to initially lower their defenses with you is to act charming. Do not act all weird and slimy with them but adopt a natural witty charm, the kind reserved for your principal or favorite high school teacher back in the day. This is especially effective with shy or insecure targets, people who would welcome compliments and are more likely to warm to jokes and strangers faster.

Another way is to break down the trust barrier by offering a little of yourself and your secrets first. This part of you doesn't necessarily have to be true but it must be believable. Once the primary connection is formed however, it is time to begin information gathering. If your mark is talkative, you are in luck. Simply keep quiet and let the prattle run. There is bound to be at least a tidbit of information scattered in between. However, if the target is more reserved or quieter, a little bit of skillful prodding is needed to tap into the right vibe and once you get it, be sure to keep the buzz going for as long as possible.

Other than information garnered from conversation, you can also proceed to watch the crowd he/she hangs out with, her favorite drinks, favorite color and hobbies. This might seem very banal but knowledge of them could give you an in with the mark and that's all that is needed to improve your status in their lives. Once you have established the right relationship, the next step is to hunt for the more private bits of information, the ones most likely to push the buttons you need pushed.

OBSERVING AND TRANSLATING EMOTIONAL REACTIONS

To properly observe a person's reactions and understand the logic or motive behind them, you have to take an objective perspective of the person's actions, devoid of any connections whatsoever. To do this you first have to establish the nature of the events or situations causing such a reaction to check for its conventionality because since most people tend to react conventionally to certain things, the abnormalities and oddities are the ones to look out for. Next, you analyze the markers of these reactions in the person so that if such a reaction were to occur for another stimulus, it would be clear what such a person is feeling. Some emotions may possess the same marker and would therefore require secondary markers or experience with the target to tell them apart.

The need for marking the emotional reaction of the target as well as its causes is to be well placed to use the emotions to your advantage. Also knowing the tells would expose to you the presence of a particular emotion, allowing you to adapt to the mood and needs of the person thus keeping yourself relevant while making them believe that you care. This might probably only be necessary at the beginning of the association as the person is more likely to show more subservience or dependence as the manipulations grows deeper.

Deciphering and translating the emotions of a person might seem tricky at first but usually gets easier with time. For instance, staying with a new cousin, family relative or roommate might be difficult at first but as you start to warm up to them and learn about their eccentricities, what makes them tick and what kills their buzz, their secrets begin to up to you one at a time. It's the same way with targets of manipulations; you need to invest time in understanding and learning their reactions and what they mean so as to avoid pushing the wrong buttons at the wrong times.

LEARN TO TAKE A CLUE

Very rarely, you might encounter an oddity that more or less does not conform to the reading you have arrived at on a particular person, do not fret and do not react too swiftly. It is better to ignore it outwardly while watching for signs of repetition. The smart play would be to analyze it, try to understand what brought about the anomaly and if it is likely to happen again. This is necessary because manipulation is about control of not only the target but of everything affecting the target that can be controlled. Those that cannot be controlled should be predicted and skillfully avoided to prevent any surprises from occurring.

Take for example, you have cultivated a manipulative relationship with a young lady or man who is quite reserved and is more prone to long periods of silence. Then on a night out together, the target completely flips script and goes all wild partygoer on you, do not react hastily. It could be as a result of something or someone in their life that you are not familiar with and a hasty reaction against a previously entrenched stimulus could be rather counterproductive. Instead, it would be advisable for you go along with the flow and later question their behavior. This would enable you to gain the knowledge you want without relinquishing control of the situation.

This is the idea behind taking a clue. You have to be ready to adapt and shift your position to better understand a situation.

TO REACT OR TO OBEY: THE KEY TO ALWAYS GETTING IT RIGHT

This is one of my favorite rules because it requires patient thinking and smart decision making. The translation is rather simple. To react is to adopt an active approach while to obey is to do otherwise. The rule applies to you, the manipulator, and the target. It is simply used to stop impulsive action. The question is quite straightforward, do you react to a situation or let things slide?

This question is one you should never fail to ask yourself before putting another ploy in motion. It would be reckless of you if you were to move too fast and sloppy of you if you were to move too slowly. That is where the question comes in. It challenges you to consider your status and decide if any further action is necessary. Failure to make the right choice often ends in regret.

An alternative question, mostly used at the beginning of a manipulation to better gauge the chances of success of the ploy, is to ask yourself how smart your target truly is. This might seem ordinary but for you to succeed you have to have complete faith in your own abilities while steering clear of overconfidence and most times a good perception of the targets own intellect is the perfect constraint.

As effective as this rule could be, there is no trick or shortcut to knowing the answer to the question. To react or to obey could only be answered by you. You are to put every piece of information you possess on the target into play and then consult your gut and instincts on whether one or the other is the right choice. You would probably stumble a few times during the learning process but you could also be a natural, getting it right every single time. Whichever it is, remember to always learn from your experiences because only through our experiences are we ever truly equipped to deal with the future.

PRACTICE MAKES PERFECT

As previously stated, manipulation has to be worked at constantly to attain the level at which success becomes the norm. Practice and constant use of the skills you learn would sharpen your skills as regards people and how they should be dealt with. All the advice in this book are merely words on a piece of paper or an audio recording without your own ability to bring them to life. Everyone is different and as such, different methods work for them. This applies to you as much as it applies to your target. You have to be able to bring the ideas in this book in a way that suits your character and approach and there is no better way to learn to do this than by practicing.

Manipulation is a game that deals with emotions and constant practice is perfect to boost your instincts as well as your confidence. Stick to these rules and warning and it's only a matter of time before you become a master manipulator. Just like in every other field, without sharp instincts, you are ordinary, without experience you carry a large chance of failure, without confidence you can do nothing. Practice is important if you are to achieve all three and rise above being ordinary.

CHAPTER 4

UNDERSTANDING BASIC BODY LANGUAGE

When two people meet each other, it doesn't matter whether they are old friends or new acquaintances, they could even be strangers, but they communicate through not only words but gestures. These gestures tend to betray our mental state and express how we are feeling. For instance, if were feeling bad and irritable, we give off defensive signals and when we are feeling happy, we tend to be more relaxed and friendlier.

These gestures and signals relay our mood to the person or persons around us and affects what they think and how they relate with us at that moment in time. This ability to read basic and common gestures is rather inherent in every one but as a result of practice and experience some people are more adept at it than others. For example, women are generally more perceptive to gestures than men, probably due to the fact that they might have had lots of practice dealing with their kids or those of others.

Many common gestures such as crying, laughing and frowning denote the same emotional and mental state in most people with very little exceptions. However, your emphasis on body language and gestures as a manipulator should go beyond the study of the more common gestures if you hope to become a master. It should at least encompass the knowledge of basic body language for you to truly appreciate its effect on your everyday choices and decisions. You should also be able to notice and translate a wide range of uncommon expressions.

Gestures and signals could mean many things in different places, so it would be wise to observe the general trends around wherever you stay and ask questions when necessary before jumping to needless conclusions. Furthermore, the frequencies with which these gestures occur vary with a variety of factors. One of these is age. It has been proven that the older people get the lesser the gestures they use in communicating their opinions. Another factor is wealth or social class. It has also been noticed that people higher up the social chain in a particular environment use fewer gestures than those below them. These are all generalizations and exceptions to such are bound to occur. For example, people who are very excited tend to gesticulate more and those who are bored, take on a more reserved demeanor. Thus, a bored teenager could probably use less gestures and body movement in expressing him or herself than an excited septuagenarian. In such a case, the age generalization would have failed.

Well, other than these generalizations, it is important to pay attention to the particular gestures of each person while also monitoring their verbal output. Look for contradictions that give the person away as regards whether they are lying or hiding something and make your next steps based on these deductions. The most effective way of catching lying in a person is to watch out for gestures that betray their true intention. Such gestures or behaviors are usually out of place or out of sync with the message they are delivering or trying to deliver.

UNDERSTANDING FROM LESS THAN WORDS

The ability to tell as much as possible about a person without engaging in conversations is one that would help you well, especially when it comes to securing and developing a new target. When I say developing a target, I mean the first few conversations and meetings you have in which you try to determine the attitude and emotional disposition of the person towards key issues so as to better mold the character you would assume around them.

This understanding of a person could aid your quest in many ways. It could portray you as someone who is perceptive and sensitive to their need and this is a good way of establishing trust within the target. It could also be useful in predicting the actions of a person so as to better react to them. This reaction could be in many forms varying from a modified approach to a subject to a complete avoidance of another. It is, in summary, a good way to avoid falling afoul of a person before you have been able to achieve what you initially set out to achieve.

Many signs could actually mean more than one thing and should not be taken as a complete truth but rather as a possible truth. What this means is that, all possible translations should be considered before you jump to any final conclusions. This is due to the fact that more than one factor could be in play and probably the telling factor causing a particular reaction is not even from us but from another person or situation entirely. Such consideration should apply to both positive and negative reactions because we, as humans, tend to apply this to only the negatives while imagining all positive reactions to be of our own making. I am going to consider the reactions we should or could expect in a first meeting because I assume that after the first meeting, your status or likely status should be established already. Let us begin with reactions to expect in a first meeting.

1. Acceptance and rejection: Being able to perceive whether someone is digging you or accepting your approach is quite important as it tells you a lot about the success of your current approach on the person and whether or not you may need to change it. Though it is very difficult to know if your message is getting through, little gestures such as moving closer and interrupting every now and then to put in a point should bolster your confidence that your presence is at least not unwanted. In fact, if you really want to judge whether or not your company is pleasing to the person, it would be more apt to look for the signals of rejection rather than those of acceptance. You should look for signs such as how regularly the person offers an opinion during a conversation, how frequently and how sincerely the person smiles or laughs at your jokes, whether the person retreats whenever you move closer and how long the person spends in a side conversation with another friend before returning to you and whether or not they apologize.

The regularity with which the person offers opinions show how much the person is concentrating on your words and this in turn denotes if and how interesting your company is. If the person speaks only a little, it could mean that the person doesn't like you or is bored. Anyhow, if walking away is not an option, you could resort to asking a question and using the persons answer to change the topic. Watch out for changes in their reactions to gauge their concentration.

Someone who laughs frequently and sincerely at your jokes is definitely enjoying the conversation and is less likely to leave soon. However, someone who just stares at you after a joke or gives a weak smile is probably not impressed by you or your wit. But before jumping to conclusions, the blank stare could also be as a result of a lack of understanding on their part.

If after a few moments of a conversation, you attempt to lean in to emphasize a point and the target (mostly females in this case) retreats, taking a step or two back, it could mean that she doesn't like you, she still considers you a stranger, she is surprised or she simply isn't feeling the conversation as much as you thought. it might even be due to mouth odor. The trick with dealing with this is to stay calm and pretend not to notice this. Continue with the conversation as naturally as possible and after a few minutes, attempt to lean in again. If she retreats again, it is probably due to one of the first two possible reasons or the mouth odor.

During conversations with a person, it is quite common for side conversations with a passing friend to occur. The duration of this side conversation could however be of significance when it comes to determining how they view you. If the side conversation goes on for so long that you look and feel like you are standing all alone and yet the person with whom you were conversing hasn't offered an apology, the meaning is quite bad. But if the person constantly cuts short the side conversation to apologize to you an even takes the hard decision of cutting short and postponing such a conversation, it means your presence is at least appreciated and not unwanted. If the former was actually the case, it could be due to the fact that the target considers your presence to be boring, and the side conversation to be a needed reprieve. If this is so walk away and do not return, unless the target approaches you. Save your dignity.

2. Happiness: Someone who immediately warms up to you in a first meeting or conversation and is happy to have your company would most likely participate in the conversation, not just butting in to express opinions but also to tell stories and crack jokes. Such a person is also likely to laugh a lot and may even attempt to introduce you to a few more people if you are a stranger at whatever place you are meeting. It is also possible that the person is intoxicated and their overly positive reaction is due to whatever intoxicant they might have ingested. The best way to deal with this is to go on with the flow and probably try getting their contact information for a future meeting but keeping whatever conclusions you may have had aside for when such a meeting comes. A distant possibility is that they are utilizing your company to achieve a goal of their own, say, making someone jealous. I classified this as a distant possibility because it rarely happens but I still felt the need to mention it so as to stress the need for you to always consider all options and to always stay aware of everything going on around you and your target.

3. Distaste or dislike: This is different from rejection in that the person in this case would probably not even be polite enough to answer you properly. It is rather easy to spot and could include signs like a frown, lack of eye contact and short or monosyllabic answers. If this happens to you, do not inquire as to what might be wrong or what you might have done wrong. Instead, say your goodbyes and walk away. If you are to approach such a person again, be sure to have a friend of theirs there to introduce you first. This could make all the difference.

The possible scenarios are endless but these are the most popular reactions you could come up against. The reason for outlining these situations and how to deal with them is to enable you use the knowledge of basic body language and how to properly react to them to better make a first conversation or meeting as fruitful as possible. If dealing with failure and rejection is not a strong point of yours, it might be better to watch from a distance how such a person relates with others and judge using these same skills, how to approach such a person or if he or she is worth the stress.

THE LITTLE THINGS ARE USUALLY MOST IMPORTANT

We have touched on some of the more elaborate and obvious gestures and the little ones are up next. These are called little because they are mostly imperceptible and are done very quickly. They are those things one is likely to miss or overlook such as a quick lick of the lip, a glance at a wristwatch or clock, a glance at another person or even running a hand through their hair. These things are likely to possess meanings that are particular to different people and as such, the same meaning might not apply to different people. These types of reactions should not be studied and translated as individual events or reaction but instead as a part of a larger one.

To adequately guess the meaning to this sort of reactions, you need to consider other gestures that might have come immediately before it, what the target was saying at the moment of the reaction and any possible contradictions between the two. The truth is such reactions rarely occur only once. Most times they are conditioned reflexes in the person to help them deal with something they are otherwise uncomfortable with. It is equally as rare for anyone to recognize any of these reactions not to talk of translating it without spending a tremendous amount of time with the person. For this reason, such reactions are psychological gold and should be cherished.

These inherent reactions are what we call tells.

RECOGNIZING TELLS AND SIGNS COULD BE AN ART OR SCIENCE

The ability to instantly recognize a tell or sign in a person when you see one could be an in born or a developed attribute. one could simply spend a few weeks with people and be able to reveal three or four tells that point to how the target is really feeling while other spend years and still struggle to recognize one. This is no reason to worry because while the ability to notice and translate tells makes manipulation easier, the absence of such a skill doesn't make it impossible. Having said this, it should be noted that recognizing such tells can be learnt so, if you lack the natural knack for seeing them, you can still manipulate your target but knowing how to recognize some would definitely be advantageous.

Some tells could be the tendency for a person to run his or her hands through the hair, crossing of the fingers, rapid blinking, twitching of the eye, rapping the knuckles on a surface and many others. These seem like actions that denote rather obvious emotions but most tells are. The major issue with a tell is that these obvious actions do not actually follow an easily perceivable emotion and are usually done so quickly, they could be mistaken for necessary. Thus, to notice them, one must be observant and to translate them, you might have a good grasp of whatever situation them might have occurred under. Isolating the situation and breaking it down into a list of potential stimuli could help in narrowing down the possible meanings.

RECOGNIZING A TARGET

One of the most important things for being a good manipulator is the ability to notice the right people, the ability to pick the right targets. Well, sorry, there are no right targets. The truth is that everyone can be manipulated by a master but it takes a lot of practice to become a master and as such, for beginners like you, picking the easy or more susceptible targets is the smarter move.

Generally speaking, the easiest people to manipulate are usually those with low self-esteem, low self-confidence or other form of insecurities. These traits usually manifest in numerous forms and it is these forms you have to be trained to notice.

- **Naivety:** This is a very popular draw for manipulation because the victim is almost never aware that he or she possesses such a trait and this limits the possibility that they will eventually discover you. It could be noticed clearly in people who always strive to see the best in others. Such a person even when confronted with the idea and even evidence of manipulation is likely to still believe everything is a coincidence and should have another explanation. This is definitely one you should look out for.

- **Emotional dependence:** People who exhibit this trait are almost always in relationships and such relationships are almost always ending. Why is this? Because their happiness depends on the happiness of others and due to this, they could be considered needy. But their neediness is to your advantage. These sorts of people would do anything to keep you happy, even if it goes against their best interests and the best thing is, they'd do it quite willingly. This would mean little effort from you and an almost servile target. The only caveat to this type of person is that, they are mostly always the jealous types. Be careful.
- **Low self-confidence:** If you have ever met someone with low self-confidence, you'd agree with me that they are always seeking validation of their actions and decisions and these tend to expose them to manipulation. As a manipulator, your power over this class of people lies in your approval and the way you use it. Withholding such an approval makes them eager, to please and giving the approval makes them happy, relaxed and ripe for the taking.
- **Pseudo-manipulators:** Have you ever met people who like to feel like they are the smartest and the most powerful in the room? If yes, this is their class. People like this usually feel like they can prey on others and are good manipulators but in truth are nothing but failures. They are very hard to find but if you ever meet a person who acts out manipulative tendencies but possesses no real influence on people, you have your mark. The way to handle such people is to play the victim or subordinate and strive to avoid doing their wishes while making sure they do yours. This might involve a whole lot of acting and a few concessions at the beginning but would definitely be worth the hassle at the end. These people are mostly narcissists and are easy to pick out using this very trait.
- **Lack of assertiveness:** These kinds of people do not have the ability to make up their mind and this is a weakness to take advantage off. You should strive to play the role of bully or higher authority, someone who makes decisions for them.

Provided you play up your best decisions while hiding your worst, you are bound to stay in their lives and stay in control.

- **Altruism:** This is one of those traits that are present in people who show a high level of honesty, fairness and empathy, emphasis on the empathy. This is the emotion to go after as it blinds the target to your true nature and makes him more likely to buy into your act. This makes he/ she susceptible to your talents but not foolish, so you'd still have to play your cards right to have the desired impact.

There are many other traits to look out for and with time and experience, you'd discover them. Looking closely, you would notice that at least one of these traits is present in everyone you know. This is the reason why everyone, even yourself can be manipulated and as such, while playing your game, never drop your guard and always be on the lookout in case your target is also playing a game on you. I should also add that while these traits make people more susceptible to manipulation, your abilities and skills are the factors that would truly determine if the manipulation would be successful or not.

WARNING SIGNS

Everybody can be manipulated but some people are less likely to fall than others. If you are a beginner and you are just learning the ropes, it is necessary for you to avoid individuals high up on the 'less likely' list. To achieve this, you need to know the particular traits or character types to look out for. Such people are:

- **The stubborn:** They are not impossible to break but are better avoided because they might cost too much effort. Stubborn people are usually hard to manipulate because they have self-created opinions, whose tenets they uphold strictly. Worse is the fact that they are prone to arguing a lot and seeing as this is rather inherent in them, it is a trait you would have to figure a way around if you plan on sticking

around. Except you are very confident you can get the job done, steer clear.
- **Insensitive people:** This type lacks the ability to feel much in terms of empathy or sympathy and only care about their own interests. You might think that's a good thing but remember, their wellbeing is most likely top of their worries and any sign of manipulation is sure to set off alarm bells.
- **Immature people:** Immaturity is normally a trait that should set people out for manipulation because it is a close sibling of naivety. However, most immature people possess the ability to hold grudges for a tremendous period of time and you do not want them hunting you down for hurting their feelings or stealing their properties. They tend to make very determined enemies. The stubborn also possess this tendency.
- **People with close friends and relatives:** The best targets are usually those who reside far away from most family and friends because this reduces the chances of trusted outside forces trying to undo your work. Unless, you can think of a way to wean your target off such influence or at least factor them into your plans, the ploy is going to be extremely difficult to pull off. Even if you are ready to manipulate the entire group, ask yourself if it is worth the effort.

CHAPTER 5

PERSUASION: THE PSYCHOLOGICAL THEORIES
(NEVER FAIL TO CONSIDER THE TARGET)

Persuasion is a deliberate effort to change or alter a person's opinions, beliefs or attitude toward a particular issue, situation, object or person. This is usually achieved by transmission of a message which could be verbal or symbolic.

While persuasion could be used in a manipulative sense, it is in actual sense different from manipulation. This is because, when persuading a person, he/she is usually aware of your efforts at changing their point of view and willingly or reluctantly allows you to try. In this instance, the person listens and concentrates on what you are saying and then tries to rationalize your ideas with reality before then putting whatever conclusions they come to comparison with what they previously believed.

Your role in the entire dynamic is to state your reasons for the change you are prescribing, give illustrations and evidence supporting your views and try to convince the target of your advances that your line of action or advice is their best bet. The main goal of this is getting them to switch to a state of reasoning or a product that you prefer. It is in this that persuasion resembles manipulation. Because your goal is still to push the target towards an outcome that they might ordinarily not have considered right.

The success attained in persuasion usually depends on the preconceptions held by the target and their strength, their perception of the person sharing the new message or idea, their perception of the message or idea and finally, their perception of the conclusion on offer. Upon outlining these reasons, it should be clear to you that the subject of your effort would probably possess ideas that are at least dissimilar, if not contradictory, to yours and as such the entire process would either hinge on your persuasion being very convincing or the ability of the target to meet a compromise between the conflicting ideas that would majorly mirror the changes you want.

Below are six major theories that strive to explain the way the human mind absorbs and reacts to information. Knowledge of these would greatly increase the odds of persuasion if you could pinpoint it in your target.

- **The attribution theory:** This concludes that people would either attribute actions and characters to people and object respectively either in relation to the context they are being considered in or according to their own emotional disposition.

    When they attribute using context as a guide, they are likely to come to decisions that take into consideration environment of origin and situational factors. Such is seen when a person refrains from calling a product inferior or calling a person insensitive, instead arguing that the product has been made from the best possible items available to the manufacturer and that the person is simply reacting as he has learnt to from his childhood environment.

    However, when considering their own emotional disposition, they tend to believe that whatever is convenient for them is the only right decision or approach for every other person. Consider this situation:

    You meet a person at an event or gathering and try starting a conversation with them but instead of giving you a polite audience, the person appears preoccupied with their own thoughts or acts aloof. Angered or annoyed, you walk away and when asked for an opinion on the person, you characterize them as proud, arrogant or self-important.

    In this case, the characterization you have concluded on is based solely on your emotional disposition and does not take into consideration, the situation or possible problems the other person might have. The idea is not to determine whether or not you are wrong or right but rather to analyze how you are likely to process information about people and things. You actually might be right about the person.

Another situation is when you have been accused of doing something wrong and you claim that your accusers have failed to see things from your own perspective and are only interested in their own point of view.

This is a perfect example of considering things as regards context. In this case, probably because the things said are negative, you'd notice the emphasis placed on contextual understanding of actions. There is also a slight hint of the dispositional thinking occurring simultaneously.

- **The conditioning theory**: In this case, the person is likely to do things if they are tailored and conditioned to look like their own decisions instead of as a result of coercion. This is most utilized in the advertising industry where commercials, advertisements and billboards are used to convey information that would provoke positive feelings in the population of interest. They then connect such feelings to their products thus making you feel that the product would bring such a feeling into your life. Because of this, you are more likely to purchase their product, thinking all the while that your decision was an independent one.

This is usually possible because we generally perceive things based on our emotions and are more likely to buy things because they make us feel good.

- **The cognitive dissonance theory**: Based on this theory, it is assumed that people tend to aim for consistency in their thoughts, attitudes and decisions. This is the reason why most people create principles which they strive to follow. Most people also seem intent on reconciling the contradictions as much as they can until they feel comfortable. I would give two examples on this.

Example 1

You have a very strong and deep-rooted need for canned food, either due to the laziness of having to cook meals or the frustrations at having to wait in queues for food. Then you are told that such canned meals could lead to cancer and you definitely don't want to have cancer. But you also don't want to stop eating canned food. So, instead of stopping with the habit, you comfort yourself that millions of people like you have the same habit and would never have cancer.

The cancer theory might be untrue but your eagerness to dispute the fact or at least to make the consequences seem less severe is your own way of changing your mind or at least making the facts you have just learned seem less important or true. This is one of the ways of dealing with cognitive dissonance theory.

Example 2

Imagine a criminal with a conscience. This is probably hard to imagine but they do exist. In such a situation, his or her criminal tendencies are clashing with their tender hearts and causing a bit of discomfort. Such a person is very likely dealing with his/ her problems by giving in to the rationale that a criminal and wealthy life far outweighs the benefits of having a clean conscience or good heart.

Again, I am refraining from judging whether such a rationale is sound but am more focused on the fact that the person seems to give in to a rationale that overlaps with the general aim of most people to deal with his discomfort. This is another way of dealing with the cognitive dissonance.

- **The judgement theory:** This one is very simple to grasp. It simply proposes that when faced with a new piece of information or idea a person's reaction is more or less dependent on the way he/she currently feels on the topic. What this means is that were likely to accept something that resonates with our current belief, reject something that doesn't fit in with our beliefs, or stay indifferent to something never previously considered.

  Therefore, when attempting to persuade a person, it is better to first determine their views on the topic to gauge whether or not you'd be successful and if your effort would eventually be worth it.

- **Inoculation theory:** The inoculation theory supports the view that even if previously uninterested in two points of view, once argued for, you are likely to pick the dominant point of view and stick with it. Here is an example of what I mean.

You have never watched a game of soccer in your life but one day you are relaxing on the beach and happen to find yourself stuck between two diehard soccer fans, who support rival teams. An argument begins about whose team is better and more dominant and they both turn to you, presenting their points like you are s seasoned fan and after some time ask you to judge on who's better. You obviously would pick the person with the better argument so as not to betray your own lack of knowledge on the subject. If in future another individual was to pose a question to you, inquiring as to which of those two teams is better, you'd probably find yourself arguing in favor of the choice you made then, maybe even with some of the same points that were used then.

This is the power of inoculations, the most powerful initial idea always takes root first.

- **Narrative persuasion theory:** From experience, I think we would all accept that stories have a more enhanced effect on perception and opinions than abstract advice. The attitudes and opinions of people towards objects and others tend to change when they are told compelling stories of such subjects.

  The theory simply attempts to explain the heightened effect can have on people if utilized properly. In this, the listener feels transported and this greatly affects their perception of events, making them more pronounced and vivid than they might have been if they had been expressed ordinarily and abstractly.

THE PSYCHOLOGICAL PERSPECTIVE

Ordinarily, persuading people would be difficult without the ability to properly organize and present an argument. But if inexperience in any or both of this is coupled with an inability to gauge and understand moods and stances, your task would be made many times more likely to fail.

The ability to instantly sense and recognize a person's stance on an issue is difficult, not to talk of performing the same trick on an audience. Because of this difficulty, most speakers who are attempting to introduce people to a new point of view always tend to ask questions that would enable them gauge the stance of the audience before moving on with their presentation.

Immediately after asking such questions, they usually watch out for visible reactions from members of the audience, maybe a smile to indicate a previous knowledge of the topic, sitting up to indicate interest, turning away or sighing to indicate disagreement or boredom or even a person willing to answer. These simple markers give you an idea as to how your message may be received and would help you map out a strategy of approach. It is also an effective tool as people tend to express themselves more sincerely when they do not feel particularly in the spotlight. So, if you are unsure, do not refrain from asking a few surface questions to test the waters or more aptly, to feel out the crowd.

It should also be noted that many people might give a negative reaction to one-on-one persuasion and would start arguments to further their points. The moment you realize that your attempt to persuade a particular person has deteriorated into an argument, it is advisable for you to walk away. Very few arguments occurring outside law courts ever get settled. Engaging in one would be fruitless and time consuming. That time is better spent elsewhere.

I stated earlier that manipulation is similar to persuasion in that both aim to change opinions, attitudes and actions from what they might have been to whatever you prefer and I had also stated that they differ from one another in that, persuasion is a more direct form of securing the change you desire, while manipulation requires you to operate in secret using emotional exploitation. Now, I would like to expatiate on the relationship between manipulation and persuasion or rather how persuasion can be adopted as a tool for manipulators.

This is not rocket science and needs only a simple alteration in approach to persuasion. It would require you to couple the ability to make compelling, irrefutable arguments with your ability to recognize emotional markers. Once both are in sync, you are ready to move. But why this two? The answer to that is rather simple. If you recognize an emotion to be dominant in the target and fell the need to convince, he or she to do something without outright manipulation, most likely due to the presence of friends and family, wouldn't it be better to play on such an emotion and use it as a leverage or platform with which you propel your point of view rather than just riding in without a strategy.

This is why persuasion makes manipulation look humane and might even reduce the noticeability of your ploy. It enables the manipulator, you, to touch on the emotions of a target for a reaction, but instead of making your telling moves under a shroud all the time, you adopt clever arguments and let them do the convincing for you. The trick however, is to always get the emotion right.

CHAPTER 6

PERSUASION: THE PRACTICAL

In the previous chapter, I touched upon persuasion as a whole, focusing on the definition, its differences and similarities with manipulation as well as their relationship and how they could be adapted to work to your benefit as a manipulator. Other than that, the means by which the human mind absorbs and relates to new information and facts was also discussed. Now, I wish to approach how the theories of information absorption can be used to your advantage in real life situations. I want to give you practical tips on how to persuade people to do your bidding effectively.

PUTTING THE THEORIES INTO PRACTICE

The theories from the previous chapter were very explanatory regarding how people are most likely to relate with information but said very little about how to take advantage of their tendencies. This should give more detailed tips and tactics as to how the theories can be used maximally in real life situations as well as the groups of people most likely to possess each attribute.

- **Use of the attribution theory:** This theory manifests in all people but is more noticeable in pseudo manipulators or arrogant people. Such people are less likely to ever accept being wrong and are more likely to blame it on perspective instead. Here is an example on hoe to deal with such people.
  Your target is a pseudo manipulator, one who likes to feel in control and powerful, and the roles in the relationship are already well defined. If on a given occasion such a person were to shut down your views in a bid to bully you into submission. You could use such an opportunity to play for

something you need. Firstly, you have to avoid arguing your point for too long or too strongly. Always put up a little resistance to emphasize their power over you. Once he/she has lapsed into the role you want for them, ask them for tips on how to do what they want from you. Be sure to keep them talking, constantly asking questions and subtly driving the conversation towards your need. When they are at the their most vulnerable, they would be ready to do anything just to keep emphasizing their power.

The thing about such targets is that they are convinced of their powers over you and believe themselves to be infinitely smarter. People who think themselves smart love nothing more than giving lectures, in which your only role is to listen and ask more questions. Once you have got them talking for an extended period, proceed to move them in your direction of interest and when they appear to feel at their most powerful, they are likely to grant it without much consideration, much like the kings of old.

- **Use of the conditioning theory:** In a real-life situation, this theory involves using your wit and humor to flatter the target into believing whatever you want them to. It also makes them more likely to consider your suggestions. This follows the general principle that you would aim to acquire more of what pleases you and in this case who. A typical example is the confident guy who prides himself on being able to pick up a different girl every night. How does he do it? He simply wows and impresses them with a combination of humor, wit, an interesting conversation and a smoothness and style that is very difficult to recreate. He basically makes them feel good for five minutes at the bar and they believe he would make them feel equally as good for the entire night and therefore, happily follow him out. Though this works on almost everyone, naïve people are bound to be more success.
- **Use of the cognitive dissonance theory:** this is a generally difficult theory to use because, the onus is usually on the targets to make all the difference on their lives. But, if properly played, and you act as the adviser and close friend

who gives the alternative idea or compromise that helps them deal with their dissonance, it makes you a sort of confidante. This gives you a choice position in their lives as from their point of view, you understand them more than any other person. This is, however, the sort of relationship that must be cultivated for a period of time before making your move.

- **Use of the judgement theory:** People rich in self-confidence, arrogant and who consider themselves smarter than most tend not to listen to or take into consideration arguments of other that are contradictory to their own views. If such people are to be persuaded, the new opinions they are to be inoculated with have to be similar to their previous ones or else all hopes would of persuading them would be impossible.

If you are to ever convince them that what they believe is wrong or inferior to yours, you need to make it feel that acceptance is their idea and not a necessity. The first step would be to pander to them, to defer slightly to their intelligence. Next, you draw similarities between your idea and theirs. When it comes to convincing, you are better served by an indirect approach where you ask questions and wait for them to answer, before gently expressing your objections, making sure to always be gentle and let their thought processes do the job of convincing them. It could be a change of opinion or a need to persuade them that a course of action better serves their interests, this method is sure to soften them up better than arguing with them.

Consider that friend who sees himself or herself as an authority on every subject regardless of how little knowledge they actually possess on the issue and remember how such people almost never back out of arguments but instead keep going at it till the environment of the discussion becomes toxic.

We have all had this kind of friend and the mistake of arguing with them even makes it harder for them to ever change their views. This is because, once they have taken a public stance an opinion, it is difficult for them to ever take another or even act against what they have supported, even if they later see more sense in your own view. This is because, going back on their belief is against their sense of pride and their ego. Thus, persuading such people is better done in private, if anything, because it gives you a chance to try again if you fail the first time. It also gives them a chance to adopt your idea in public without looking weak or stupid.

- **Use of the inoculation theory:** This is easy to utilize because almost everyone is susceptible to this. The key is making sure the person as no previous beliefs or opinions on the issue at hand. That is the only criterion. Once you are sure of this, you explain to them the advantages of your views. Never forget to also share the disadvantages but do this in a way that it doesn't affect the message you want them to have. The reason why the disadvantages must be made clear is that if they associate what you have explained to them with lies later along the line, they are very likely to change their views as a whole. So, if you need such people for the long term, make sure they have the full gist. Always emphasize the advantages and play down the disadvantages but never conceal them. This is as such, less a matter of persuading a person as it is initiating belief in them. For this reason, knowledge and utilization of this theory could be very powerful in the right situations. Such a situation is when you find yourself pitching a unique and previously utilized business idea in a meeting or when trying to preach a new doctrine, be it religious, academic or technological.
- **Use of the narrative persuasion theory:** The power of stories is well known. If you doubt it, all you have to do is think about how evangelists and religious clerics preach their messages. Are you getting the idea now? Though I should probably say that these clerics are probably among the most trained persons in the art of persuasion Because at one point they make use of so many theories of persuasion, constantly changing their tactics to better fit your fears and worries. But, enough with the clerics. The narrative persuasion theory is perhaps the most effective at persuading people because it

involves giving them a story, a character that they could relate to and then relying on that story to do your convincing. Such a story might be true or if you are very talented, made up.

It really doesn't matter as long as you can get them to listen. It might not work every time when used alone but if you were to mix it up with other theories, just like the clerics, the chances of success are better.

OTHER TECHNIQUES OF PERSUASION

Persuasion, like manipulation, possesses guidelines on how best to achieve your aim. These guidelines could be treated as strategies or tactics and would increase your chances of success the more you get used to them. The faster, the better.

- **Use of force:** The use of force or aggression could be effective or not and more often than not, it is a win or nothing tactic. It involves not a lot of coaxing but a lot of demanding and as such, if the person or audience don't dig the vibe, there is no other means of retreating. It usually involves use of statements that sound threatening and would most likely be a good fit for dealing with people with low self confidence and sense of self-worth. Also note that if the idea is to impress friends and family of your target, it would be better if this tactic were used in private beyond the hearing or view of other parties as it could easily be perceived as bullying.
- **Commitment and consistency:** These are highly respected values in the minds of most people in all walks of life. When coupled with a little bit of success, it could be very effective if not the most effective means of persuasion. If you want someone to believe your way is gold and your opinions are equally as rich, there is no better way than providing an example of their successes. In most cases, the best example is usually yourself. Showing commitment to your ideals and consistently applying them successfully tends to convince people of their truthfulness. It eliminates the need for you to

continue arguing your points regularly, instead let them persuade themselves that following your example is the right thing. It would be like seeing a successful person and emulating them in the hopes that you'd achieve their level of success the same way. We all do it, so why not use it to our advantage when dealing with others.

Another angle to this, could be to get the target to commit themselves to promises or writing. This would be useful because most people care about reputations and rarely want to be seeing going back on their words. While this second angle would be an effective tool on arrogant people and pseudo manipulator, the first method is more likely to work for people lacking in confidence and self-esteem.

- **Social influence:** Social influence could manifest in one of two ways. It could be positive or negative. Positive influence would point to the need for one to follow the convention or approach that is the most common around him/her or among friends. The negative influence, on the other hand deals with the tendency of people to act against the norm. The influence that is expressed is usually deep rooted and expresses itself in more than one fact of the target's life. Once the targets tendency has been established, you could move to surround the person only with people who possess the approach that would produce the result you desire. This method is also applicable to people with a low sense of self-esteem and confidence.
- **Action by reciprocity:** reciprocity generally means the need or tendency to give back when you are given something. You are probably wondering how this affects persuasion, right? This is straightforward. Giving something creates the need in the target to give back. This in turn is a weakness that makes the target more susceptible to catering to a need that they otherwise could have overlooked. This is also applicable to arrogant people as well as those who possess altruistic dispositions. An empathetic person is also likely to fall for such a ruse. This could also be used or claimed to be used

subliminally, as most times you need not even state the need verbally or outrightly but instead subtly imply to its absence.

- **Use of authority or sternness:** If the target is a naïve person or one who is lacking in decisiveness or assertiveness, this is the ideal method of approach. This is for people who are prone to listening to other people's opinions and taking it for the truth, especially when they consider the person to be more of an authority on the subject than they are. It would also help if they consider your views trustworthy and knowledgeable. This is the method of choice when dealing with a new or junior colleague or at least someone who is new to an environment and is not yet well versed in how things operate. However, treating such people could also be counterproductive, causing them to view you in a negative light.

- **Taking advantage of love:** It might be a simple crush or a big attraction, but people almost always say yes to people they like and feel something positive for. So, if you have a target that you feel is attracted to you, play their feelings to your advantage and ask for whatever you want, just be careful to give a little back and do not overdo it. If the person is emotionally dependent on you, your luck is strong because they are even less likely to utter a word for fear of losing you to another. The best part is that they never realize that such is happening, as it is a very natural reaction.

- **Leveraging your trust and integrity:** if you are generally acknowledged to be trustworthy, you are more likely to be believed. This could be done by smartly showing off your impeccable reputation, if you have one, while avoiding the line of arrogance. That could spoil the effect. Another way to use this tactic is to put your character in the spotlight, if you have a good one, and making sure to back up your every point with a vow of assurance in its trustworthiness.

The last is to give a sense of expertise. Show that you possess more knowledge than they do and when added to your reputation and character, you have a cocktail of persuasion that even the most steadfast of non-believers would

reconsider. It is also likely to work on naïve people and people who consider themselves intellectual.
- **Making use of sympathy and empathy:** These two emotions can easily be manipulated because they usually convey on their owners, a sense of innocence and docility that can be used against them. With the right words and gestures, you should be able to convince such people of anything. For a more advanced effect, make use of stories as such people are also prone to following the narrative transportation theory and the combination of these two factors make them better candidates to believe than most.

REVERSE PSYCHOLOGY

Reverse psychology is a technique of persuasion where a speaker or person utilizes a behavior or idea that is contradictory to that which he wants to occur. The user of this technique does or asks for the opposite of what they actually require of the target, encouraging the target to do as they wish.

This works on people who make a habit of resisting authority. If tried on people who are more agreeable, they might and would probably do as you have asked. For this reason, they do not make good candidates or targets for reverse psychology to be used upon.

However, even when used with resistant people, reverse psychology should be used as subtly as possible because no one enjoys or likes being manipulated and as such, if they recognize what you are doing, it is likely you would not achieve much with them. An example of the use of reverse psychology is advising someone to do something when you know that the very idea of the advice infuriates him/her and would probably push them towards doing the opposite. The idea is usually to establish the idea you actually want them to absorb then play it up subtly to become tempting, before changing tack and arguing against it. Immediately after this, you push them to make a decision and that's all. It is likely that they would go with it because other than the fact that they would want to resist the advice, it is also the idea that they were exposed to first. It is not necessary to take such steps if you know the person well enough to understand what they like, dislike and how they would react in given situations.

REMEMBER TO ALWAYS ANALYZE BEFORE MAKING YOUR MOVE

The reason why most people fail in persuading people into a line of action is that they fail to grasp what is necessary for their success and if they do, they fail to take it all into consideration. It is for this same reason that persuading strangers is more difficult than persuading people you are closer to. Because if you were to ignore a person's emotional disposition and shelf their possible reactions, it would be the same as approaching a stranger. To really succeed at persuasion, most times you might need to adopt maybe a dominant, authoritative attitude or a more reserved one.

When being authoritative, you have to give off a vibe of knowledgeability and confidence. You must convince the person that you know what you are speaking about, while emphasizing their own knowledge. There is a loophole here. If this is tried on a resistant person, he or she is likely to do the opposite of what you advise and thus fall a victim of reverse psychology. You see that knowledge of the person is important in determining the best technique for persuasion for without it, you would be charging blindly.

You should also avoid using reverse psychology very often as such misuse could expose your tricks and make the target more immune to your ministrations. It could be particularly damaging to relationships and you do not want this, unless that in itself is your goal. If you are to use reverse psychology, always remember to stay smart and stay calm. Do not let your emotions control you but, just like in manipulation, control your emotions.

Persuasion is an art that all socially influential people crave possession of. This is because the ability to make people do as you wish and while you can directly manipulate individuals, it becomes trickier when dealing with groups of people. But if you were to master this art, your power and influence would benefit greatly.

CHAPTER 7

COMMON MANIPULATION TECHNIQUES

At a point in our life, and at least once daily for most, we resort to manipulation to get what we want. It could be a little lie to get out of a tight spot or harmless flattery to get yourself a choice seat but it is manipulation. So, stop believing that manipulation is an art reserved for only the evilest of people, everyone does it so it's simply better to get very good at it. Though it is better to look out for some traits that predispose some to manipulation more than others, it doesn't mean that people without such traits can't be played.

I have previously elaborated on such traits as well as other means of gaining control over people but it's time to approach the real topic of discussion, how to manipulate people.

Lying

This is the most popular of all manipulation techniques. On its own, lying is simply misinforming the target or at the most, concealing information from the target but when done with a view to controlling people, it becomes a pretty powerful weapon. Consider lying as a tool to soften up a target that has until that moment proven too strong. Lying in this way would require one to betray the very intent of conventional lying because in this case, you are not trying to misinform or conceal but rather to confuse.

If you are to succeed at this, your lies need to be believable and contradictory at first. At the beginning of such a ploy, it is necessary for your lies to constantly bounce of each other, creating a means through which you could sow seeds of confusion in someone who is usually sure of themselves.

Consider lying to a partner about a past relationship. Then in a later discussion on a similar topic, drop a previously thought of slip-up that contradicts the first experiences you shared with them.

The target might not notice this at first and may require a few more similar lies before the inconsistencies start to call their attention but when it does, instead of defending yourself, clam up and play the victim. Tell a sob story about emotional pain and all of that; share with them the reason for your lies. The stories and reasons might be fictitious, but the more realistic the better. So, be sure to think everything through first.

In this sort of scenario, the initial contradicting lies are needed to throw a seemingly strong person off balance. There is nothing like a perfect person or a truly balanced person and, as such, regardless of how strong we might seem on the outside, we all have weaknesses and there is no better way to start the process of exposing someone's emotional vulnerabilities than forcing them to instigate a heart to heart moment or discussion. If you were to try creating such a moment on your own, the target would still be likely to stay closed. However, if such a discussion is their idea, whatever barriers they possessed, they would have brought down by themselves. That is the goal with this lie.

It puts you in a position to change the narrative. In a situation in which the power was previously balanced in most of your relations, making yourself seem weak or vulnerable could put the target in an uncomfortable position and force them into opening up to adapt to their new role. Just be sure to keep any contradictory lies out of your final story. While this might not bring you much in terms of favors, having them belief you opened up on some deep secret to them strengthens their attachment. they feel a stronger bond has been formed. This trick is likely to work on people who are emotionally secure and need to believe you are really open with them before they can open up.

Punishment

When I say punishment, I do not mean physical abuse or violence. No, I mean resorting to tactics like the silent treatment, nagging, shouting or mood swings. I know you are probably thinking how any of these behaviors could get you any control but if you learn to selectively release such emotions and actions at the right time, they could exert just the right effect on the target.

The silent treatment for example could be used to put the right person in a state of wanting to please you. This treatment is a popular one for manipulators when dealing with assertive people as well as people with low self-confidence. In such case, you create a fictional quarrel in your head that need not have happened in reality. All it needs to be is believable and offensive from your perspective. Then follow through with the silent treatment. When the target gets desperate to get you back to your former self, drop the act and ask for whatever you wish for. This is a direct technique that might not always work but for a beginner, it is worth a try and for an expert, if partnered with the right set of skills and ploys, its chances of success become better.

Remember when you were little and your parents tried keeping you away from the candy or cookie jar and instead of throwing a tantrum and crying, you just stalked back to your room, threw the sheets over your head and refused to talk to anybody. You wait for hours determined not to make the first move and, later at night your parents come into the room, bearing gifts and treats and maybe even the promise of a trip you want.

Not all children did this but most did and yes, children manipulate too. They might not recognize it for what it is but they actually do it and since it works, they keep resorting to it again and again. The best thing about such a ploy is at the exact instance during which it occurs, the target believes that they are doing the right thing to keep you happy and keep the relationship from dying.

If nagging were to be the strategy of choice for you. Be sure the target is either one who lacks assertiveness or one who is eager to please because such people are likely to react favorably to nagging. Let's say you want something badly, all you have to do is keep asking and asking until they give in. Due to their lack of assertiveness, through all the asking, they would probably never give you an outright no for an answer and if it is a target who is always eager to please, he or she would have begun considering the pros and cons from the second time you ask and with just a little extra push, they would cave.

Mood swings are another very effective strategy in unbalancing a target. They are just more negative than lying and if utilized, care has to be taken to avoid dwelling too much or for too long on negative emotions such as anger. rather, it would be better to spend more time in a neutral state of boredom or indifference. The trick behind utilizing mood swings is to make your target associate some actions of theirs with particular moods of yours. This would give them an idea about what you like and dislike without you uttering a word. It is thus, advised to use this tactic alongside a more reserved attitude.

Imagine your roommate tends to leave their dishes undone after a meal, you do something drastic like throwing such plates in the trash and then refrain from talking much about it for that night but when you wake the next morning, you adopt a lighthearted demeanor and refuse to lower the smile regardless of what he or she does.

The next time, your roommate invites someone over without informing you and you act in a similar way. You never let your reactions slip over into the next day and other than when the target does something you find offensive, never react in such a way. Also, make sure that you do this only rarely.

Depending on the type of person your roommates is he or she would react differently. If the person is naive or is lacking in self-esteem, they would pander to you and fail to repeat whatever it is you reacted to but if the person is insensitive, your reactions would probably not do the trick and you would have to resort to another tactic.

Sarcasm and flattery

While other techniques mentioned earlier have dealt with manipulation using actions and acting, if you are good with words, this is a more likely weapon for you. The power of words is often underexaggerated in favor of actions. However, if mastered, they could be just as useful if not more.

Sarcasm and flattery are two slightly contrasting techniques that could be used to control the actions and opinions of people. They are usually most effective on someone who lacks self-esteem. Such a person is likely to believe most negative and positive things you say about them and start working to please you. Because of this, you could use sarcasm to deliver well planned putdowns whenever such a person offends you, only to resort to flattery to increase their confidence. Such polarity on such a week mind means they would cling to you for the compliments and flattery and would start doing things only to please you even if it goes against their own needs.

The applications of sarcasm and flattery lose all or at least most of their effectiveness if they are blatantly employed. To avoid these you must understand the need for subtlety. In the case of sarcasm, the very idea is for you to be blatant in your execution while subtly hiding your goal. You must make whatever comment you deem fit without making the target feel as if you are directing them towards a particular line of action. Failing at this could have the alternate effect of making them immune to you.

When you were young, you probably associated bullies with violence, shoving people into lockers and all but you should be able to point out that person who always alternated in behavior, showing you his or her good parts on one day, only to switch it up the next. The person would have been so polarizing that people were often confused about whether they loathed or loved him or her and with time would start to find that they hovered around such people, trying to cater to their every need. Do you recognize them now? You probably had a few in your high school and most times they were really popular.

Two of the most effective tactics employed by those people were sarcasm and flattery. With subtle swipes of their tongues they could play down your happiest moment or your biggest achievement to be something worthless and in the next, they could make one of your more ordinary actions seem spectacular. As much as they hurt your feelings, you'd still find yourself doing things they would find pleasing whenever they were around.

This might have happened to you and it might not have but the very fact that it happened to some speaks volumes of the effectiveness of such tactics. So, never forget to destabilize a mark using sarcasm and flattery. Another advantage of these two techniques is that they keep you from having to resort to trickier aggressive or abusive techniques when slight words and gestures would do the trick perfectly.

Isolation

This is mostly a secondary tactic used to make sure no external forces mess with your manipulation. The presence of family and friends around the target provide an extra level of insulation or protection around the target as such people tend to call the target back on some of their actions when they get suspicious. Their presence there, whispering into the ear of the mark thus creates another source of influence, besides yours, whose sole purpose is to thwart your influence.

Whenever you get the target to fulfil a need for you such people would call he/she back and try to expose how you are manipulating them and that puts the ploy you have implemented in jeopardy.

On its own, isolation is not that effective but it is worth noting that in the absence of friends and family alike, the target starts to look onto you as their only source of advice, comfort, love, help etc. In other words, they become completely dependent on you emotionally and this heightens the level of control you possess over them. This in turn makes them easier to influence.

Guilt tripping and love bombing

These two are a very common duo used by manipulators but that doesn't in any way affect their effectiveness. Guilt tripping is when you manipulate your targets reactions making them feel guilty about doing particular things simply by playing on their emotional vulnerabilities. Naturally, guilt is a very uncomfortable feeling which most people strive to eliminate. This need to eliminate their guilt after an incident is what you should aim to take advantage of. Since such chances might be few and far between, the initiative to create situations that give you a platform on which you could leverage a person's guilt against them is on you. In such a case, the understanding of your targets emotions and what makes them tick comes into play. You need to know how you can make them feel guilty so as to take advantage of them and their guilt.

Consider a situation in which a partner or girlfriend refuses to accompany you to a company gathering. If the gathering is not important to you, you could clam up and use a mood swing to leverage them for something that is. But if you consider the gathering too important to miss or you need a plus one to impress a particular attendee and your partner is refusing. You could play the guilt card, making them feel selfish and unkind for not considering your needs. You would make yourself the victim, putting your partner in an awkward position where they feel like they are depriving you of something you need for their own selfish reason. When this is used on less assertive people or people lacking in self-confidence, the result is usually stunning as more often than not they end up doing exactly what you want. They might even outperform your expectations simply because of their need to eliminate the feelings of guilt you have created in them.

Using such a tactic, you rile up someone that loves or is attached to you by telling them and claiming that they do not care or are too selfish in the way they treat you. This would keep an emotionally vulnerable person in check, making them see you as the victim of their actions a rather than the other way around. They would then be eager to prove your claims wrong, thus, increasing in them the need to please.

Love bombing, on the other hand, is a technique in which you continuously and over an extended period of time shower a person with love, impressing them with charm while getting whatever you want from them. This is usually much difficult to tell apart from real love and that's what makes the mark even more vulnerable. Love bombing is effective on almost everyone because as humans we all love to feel good and this need drives our selection of the people we hang out with. If someone makes us feel loved and cared for, we impulsively strive to spend more time with them. This would also mean that the target would feel more inclined to satisfy your need in order to maintain his or her happiness. However, like most tactics, the effect of love bombing is more pronounced in some character types. What this means is that, depending on the level of love bombing you expose a target to, some would see it is as a result of you trying to be nice and would consider you a good friend while other would see your actions as more and would consider you as more than a friend.

Individually, love bombing and guilt tripping are effective but when combined they are devastating. I am yet to explain reinforcement but the effect they produce is quite similar. To achieve such an effect, you should probably expose the target to your loving and charming side. Make the effect of your love felt then when the moment is right, you withdraw it and leave the target craving for it. The next step is to up the ante by making them feel guilty about your withdrawal. You make them feel like your current mood and state is their fault and when you feel that they are ripe and ready to accommodate your whims and needs, you slowly slip back into the role of loving and caring for them.

Most of the time, this works and its success is because every time you put both ploys in play, you create a sort of hypersensitivity to your needs and wants in the target. You get them into a state a where all they want to do is return to the period of time when all you did was love them and charm them.

You might also resort to completely playing the victim just to make the target more uncomfortable and guiltier, softening them up for whatever it is that you actually want of them.

This is the technique used by con men and women who want to take advantage of vulnerable people and make some wealth for themselves in the process. They inveigle their way into the lives of such people and then love-bomb them to the point where, the target cannot imagine an extended period of time without them and would, for that reason alone, do anything to keep them happy. Whenever they fail to get their way, they would then resort to guilt tripping in order to bring the target back into a state of mind in which their major thought would be on pleasing them. It might seem odd and unbelievable but if you think about it long enough, you'd realize that these two are the most used techniques by gold diggers and emotional swindlers.

Reinforcement

This technique is easy to understand but hard to actually apply and as such is better learnt by trial and error. In this ploy, you provide the target with whatever he or she wants, be it money, gifts, sex or companionship, provided it is within your capability. And after the person grows accustomed to having what you give them, you begin the process of constantly withdrawing and providing them with these, constantly keeping them on their toes and making them vulnerable with you.

The major trick here is figuring out what the target wants, what makes them tick or what most tickles their ego. You have to identify that weakness that everyone has and reinforce it. It might be praise and recognition the person desires, give it to them. It might be money and gifts, give it to them. It might be sex or prestige, give it to them. But whenever you feel they are not conforming to your whims or are not taking care of your needs or are even daring to take you for granted, withdraw all that you have given to them and in a bid to get it all back, they would come groveling and begging. After the first time, they would probably learn to satisfy your every want if they don't want you withdrawing your reinforcement.

For example, there is at least a smidgen of materialism in all of us and this can be taken advantage of. If you meet a lady whose weakness lies in her love of material possessions and you have the money to spend, you are in luck. All you have to do is charm her, take her on a few shopping trips, spend your money on her and basically reinforce her love of material things. Upon every reinforcement, try upping the ante on the things you ask of her. You could start with insisting she spend more time with you, insisting she accompany you to any event you wish and with time you could try asking her or commanding her to stay over whenever you like. To keep up the supply of riches, love for which you have reinforced in her, she would most likely conform to your needs or at least beg for a reprieve rather than reject you. But if she seems to take your kindness for granted, kick her to the curb and withdraw your reinforcement. She is likely to come back hat in hand, apologizing for her behavior and eager to please.

Not to restrict this to only your love life, this technique could also be applied to almost any setting, including business, family relationships and any case in general provided there exist a means by which you reinforce the individual or group involved. If you think about it, you would notice that there really is little difference between this and parents who threaten to ground you and take away your freedom unless you behave as they wish or business men who pull out of deals with established customers in the hope of pushing them into making desperate, unfavorable deals that would benefit them.

In the case of the parents, they have reinforced your love of freedom by allowing you do the things you like most of the time. This, when coupled with our inherent need to be free, makes us eager to please them anytime they threaten to take that freedom away. Couple the love for freedom with the fact that they are your providers of everything you need and you would see that they have quite the hold on you.

As I implied earlier, manipulation is rife in the world and silently hoping for an ideal world in which it doesn't exist would make no difference. It is better you wizen up and get better at it than other before you are taken on a ride.

I left this as the last technique on my list because there is a possibility or rather, an inevitable reaction that you always have to take into consideration when dealing with people. This is ingratitude or sometimes boredom. People tend to take for granted things they can have all the time and over a long period of time, they are bound to get bored. To avoid this, you would need to be very good at utilizing multiple techniques at various times on the same target.

This ingratitude or boredom is most likely to occur when reinforcement is used and to counter this reaction you must understand that whatever you are reinforcing in the target could make them take you for granted. Because of this, you must always be ready to withdraw your reinforcement not only when they misbehave but also when you like to. This sounds mean and selfish and it actually is, but you need to know that for reinforcement to work, you need to be selfish. You have to make the target see your needs as being more important than theirs and to successfully do this, selfishness is necessary. The target needs to know that your efforts at making them feel good come at a price and the price is anything you want in return. Thus, being nice doesn't cut it here; you need to be mean sometimes to truly make it work for you.

MANIPULATION IS NOT ALWAYS FOR THE FAINT HEARTED

Manipulation is not always wrong, nor is it always right but one thing that can be agreed upon is that it leaves an effect on both the user and the target. Depending on how manipulation was used, the effect might be positive or negative. Manipulation is usually used as a means of harming, subduing or using a person usually in a way that benefits the manipulator mostly at the expense of the target. The negative effects of manipulation are not experienced by the victim alone and in most cases, the users are not aware of the negative effects their behavior is having on their lives and, thus, become victims of their own manipulation. One of the problems of manipulation is the transfer or possession of power.

Power is naturally very addictive and very corrupting and so when faced with the question of what to use the power you have over people for, people tend to think about their selfish needs and how to make them happen. The idea of having power over a group of people or person is tempting and when such power is gotten it can lead to complete subordination and even abuse. While that is an effect on the victim, the user of such power might also become dependent on it thus making it difficult for them to have any sort of relationship with anybody unless they have power to exert. This can be damaging, both psychologically and emotionally, in the long run.

CHAPTER 8

MASTERING THE ART OF SUBTLETY-DO NOT BE BLATANT

If manipulation isn't subtle, it probably wouldn't be effective. The very idea of manipulation thrives on the ability to subtly plant ideas, thoughts and opinions in the mind of the target and frame it in such a way that they believe that such ideas are the best they could come up with or the right thing to do.

Subtlety is necessary because the target has to feel that your every action is natural and actually not intended to influence them. This would mean that you first have to reduce the frequency with which you manipulate them. Manipulating them would mean reacting regularly in a negative way to what they do. This might seem unnatural to the target and could even lead them into believing that you are always trying to push on their buttons which, by the way, you are. The ability to be subtle is as important as the ability to read emotions because subtlety makes your knowledge of their emotions and reactions remain unknown to them.

Being blatant in the way you manipulate a person would also draw the attention of other people such as friends and family and, in all honesty, there is hardly a better way to put your manipulation of a target in jeopardy than exposing them to the influence of their family and friends. The simple secret to being subtle is to keep your judgements to yourself and keep your actions and reactions as cool and as undetectable as possible.

THE CAUTIOUS APPROACH IS ALWAYS BEST

Regardless of how vulnerable a target might seem or how susceptible to manipulation they might look from a distance, it is necessary for you to approach the idea of manipulating a person cautiously. It isn't ever something to jump into just because of the possibility that the manipulation could be successful.

Cautiousness has to extend to all areas of the manipulation, from the planning to the approach and everything in between. This is especially important when dealing with strangers or people with whom you haven't spent that much time with. The emotions of such people are usually difficult to follow, even for the experts, and as such it is better to proceed with utmost caution at first and consolidate on the little progress you make.

The same thing applies when dealing with people you know because even though the chances of you getting it wrong is very slim, it still exists and for this reason you have to consider your actions before going on with them otherwise you risk destroying your relationships.

Another problem with throwing caution to the wind is that it exposes your tactics and your goal to the target. While some people might just cut you loose and move on with their lives, others might feel the need to expose you to a dose of your own medicine. Such people would probably try to manipulate you in return with a view at causing you pain. So, if the need to succeed does not make you cautious, maybe thinking about your own well-being does the trick.

A FLIMSY PLOY IS INEFFECTIVE

Other than the ability to actually go through with the manipulation, another thing to pay attention to is the solidity of the ploy. This consists of details such as the rightness of the strategy to be utilized as regards the emotional and psychological disposition of the target as well as the situation in which you find yourself in.

The technique applied always has to seem like a natural reaction to whatever situation you find yourself in. If the reaction is unnatural, the ploy might still work out but if looked at closely, what you are doing would become more visible to the target and more so to outsiders who lack the emotional dependence the target has for you.

For this reason, no matter who the target is or how long the relationship has been going on for, you always need to make sure that the manipulation is foolproof and that no one is the wiser to your plans.

Scouting out the right target and putting the right approach into play would be useless if the general ploy is easily seen through. The ploy has to consist of you yourself, the image you are portraying to the target, how the role you are playing interacts with your actions and most importantly, the fluidity of the entire ploy. If any of this is found lacking or for some reason, the various elements are found to be out of sync with one another, the chances of success reduce considerably.

NEVER GET AHEAD OF YOURSELF

The ability to keep yourself on track and put your mind to the task even when things are going well for you is an important attribute in every facet of life. Regardless of how well the relationship might be for you at a particular time or how much the manipulation is serving your interests, never ever lose track of yourself.

A loss of concentration could manifest in many ways. It could be a tendency for you to lose hold of your target, a need to avoid subtlety or the urge to fast-track a ploy. Any of these is risky as it exposes you to a better chance of failure, which in turn could lead to a complete breakdown of your plan. You must always stay alert to your surroundings and the reactions of your target to them. You must never fail to recognize how a situation affects a target or else you risk losing them prematurely.

NEVER GO ALL OUT UNLESS...

Subtlety is a rule most manipulators always conform to. The ones who choose to not obey this are often less successful and when they succeed, their success is usually short-lived. We have established the need for secrecy and subtlety but there are times when being subtle is disadvantageous or not as effective as being blatant. In these cases, you are advised to apply the needed pressure where necessary.

The ability to recognize when a situation requires more pressure than finesse as well as the best way to deliver such pressure is one garnered through experience and failure.

Situations that could call for the application of pressure are numerous but you must be able to determine if the pressure is actually necessary and how to apply it. One such situation is the need to keep a target when you feel they are slipping away.

For example, you have been working a target for a while. You have done everything by the book, maintaining isolation, staying on guard and generally looking out for any potential spoilers while getting what you want from the target. Then, in comes an old friend who is not so charmed by you. This friend goes on the attack, trying to pull the target from your clutches and you have really worked out to get to this point. You don't want to stop now. Then to bring your target back, you do something drastic like proposing marriage. This is the sort of pressure I am talking about.

In such a situation, you would agree that all other more subtle methods might and probably had already failed under such a spirited assault from the friend but instead of pulling out and walking away, you do the one thing that would express your desperation to keep the target close to you. Saying this here makes it look like showing desperation is a bad thing but from the point of view of the target, it convinces them of the truthfulness of your affection. If such a friend truly suspected of manipulation, she would have most likely used your avoidance of true commitment to prove her point and such an act would completely vilify their views and opinions in the eye of the target.

CHAPTER 9

PRACTICAL USES OF MANIPULATION

Manipulation as a tool is quite versatile as it does not particularly have any situations that it is restricted to. What this means is that, as long as people are involved in whatever you are involved in, be it a business setting, a relationship or whatever, manipulation can be used to further your agenda

MANIPULATION IN BUSINESS

the knowledge of manipulation and persuasion is critical if you plan to avoid being drawn into office politics not of your making or if you are out to avoid being cheated or railroaded by superiors and colleagues alike. Also, in business settings, there is a need for members of the same organization or group to confirm their views with one another and influence each other to cater to the group's interests. The ability to persuade people that your point of view is best would be quite handy in such a scenario.

Sales people also need to be well versed in the arts because most times they deal with people who believe them to be swindlers and for that reason they need to manipulate the persons perception of them, creating a positive one, before they could then begin the process of persuading such a customer to try out their products. there are some informal rules to follow when practicing manipulation in such business setting.

1. Don't push the limits: when I say limits, I do not mean yours, I mean that of the people you are manipulating. One of the ways that people punish the limit is by trying to manipulate everyone very time. While this might work effectively in a relationship, in an organization, everyone watches everyone closely and being associate with a tendency to manipulate people does not do your credibility much good. You have to be smart enough and disciplined enough to refrain from doing anything unless it is important. You have to always pick your battles well. If you overdo it and people start to view you as manipulator, they start to monitor your every move and even the most mundane of your actions become an object of intense scrutiny. Such scrutiny would make it a whole lot more difficult for you to achieve anything when it truly matters.

2. Sharpen your senses: Senses in this sense mean the ability to listen to and watch others. In a business setting, the ability to listen and perceive the disposition of others and so, when possible, say nothing, take a backseat and let others have the floor. Due to the fact that everybody in such a setting is always trying to get ahead of the next, it would be better if you could discern their strategies and goals, and there is no better way to achieve that by putting yourself in a position to hear and see everything.

3. Create a connection: Be it a customer or a colleague, you have to build a connection with them. Most people make the mistake of believing that they only need to build connections with their bosses but this line of action would only serve to paint you as your boss' stooge and alienate you from your fellow workers. on the contrary, forging a bond with both your colleagues and your bosses would make them see you as more of a bridge and less of a stooge. Another need for such a connection is the fact that you are more likely to be in the position to influence the thoughts and opinions of people when they feel they have a connection with you than if they consider you a complete stranger. This is particularly important when you are pitching an idea to others and its absence is the major reason why cold pitching is a very difficult trick to pull off.

4. Always stay neutral, when you can. in a business setting, neutrality should be your best strategy. Never take sides unless you have utmost confidence as to which side possesses more power. Taking sides early on would strip you of your flexibility and limit you to working only one angle. You must eb adept at playing both sides until you recognize which side would come out on top. The right way to maintain neutrality is to acknowledge the talents of everyone equally while also expressing real views regarding their failures.

Other than strengthening your position of neutrality, such a tactic would also earn you the respect of everyone. However, like every other tactic you have to know when to apply this and this knowledge would be the difference between you successfully holding you position or even advancing in the ranks and you ailing spectacularly.

MANIPULATION IN RELATIONSHIPS

Manipulation ion relationships is the one society is most sensitive about. If you manipulate in the office, most people, outsiders, would view it a s a general tactic used by many in the same situation, but manipulating in a relationship is in the eye of most, a negative marker on the character of the manipulator. Regardless of whether your intentions are pure or selfish, this opinion does not change and it is for this reason that whatever plan you have for a spouse or close friend must be done in utmost secrecy. This brings us to a previously stated point, isolation.

Isolation is one of the most important factors to be considered if you want your manipulation of a person to be successful. You must wean the target off their family and friends, establishing yourself as their confidante and emotional companion. This is because the external influence exercised by such people is capable of rivalling that which you have created and rendering your plans a waste of time.

Another thing to pay attention to is your intention. You must be disciplined, check yourself and make sure that your needs from the target do not morph into complete selfishness. You must learn to control and wield the power you possess over them with caution and with sense to avoid causing them harm. This is only possible if you think beyond your own needs and ask yourself if your need might lead to any negative consequences for the target and if so, how serious such consequences would be. Manipulation is a very powerful tool and should be treated as such.

MANIPULATING A FRIEND

Of all settings for manipulation, this is the most popular and the least suspicious or revolting. Manipulating a friend is so common, we barely pay attention to it. It usually manifests when we want to get information or something out of one another.

The best and easiest method of manipulating friends is through the use of reciprocity and compliments. Sometimes we do favors for friends because we want to but we also grant difficult favors not because we want to but because we recognize that we might need something equally as difficult to grant in the future. You do not always have to do big things, it might be a couple of smaller favors, but having them in the bag means you could leverage on reciprocity later in the future. Beware of insensitive or particularly selfish people, because they tend to not conform to reciprocity except it favors them in the moment.

The use of compliments is another way by which we unknowingly and harmlessly manipulate ourselves. The compliment might be sincere or insincere but when we give them, we recognize that they make our friends feel better about whatever it is they might have done, making them more likely to make us feel better too, whether by returning such compliments or by other means.

Offering support sort of falls under reciprocity but it is still valid as a standalone point. We might argue that offering our support to our friends in arguments and in their time of need is the right thing to do but even when we think they are wrong, we rarely ever withdraw our support. why? This is because, when we have arguments or times when we need support, we recognize the need to have someone in our corner and who better than someone who we offer unconditional support to when they need it. You can see that the manipulation is usually unintentional and harmless, but it is still a manipulation because if faced with the same choice when another person is involved, such a friend would probably do what they feel is right and not what you need. In this way, you can see that the need to reciprocate the support you showed has altered their behavior and reactions.

SEDUCTIVE MANIPULATION

Like cleopatras manipulation of both Julius Caesar and Mark Anthony, this involves using your sexuality and possible sexual prowess as a tool in getting whatever it is you need from a target. While this is an effective method, it also doesn't last that long if you can't get the target to develop more tangible feelings for you.

The truth is that there is a limit to how long sex can hold a person down and because of this, it is better to initially play hard to get. This has the double effect of making them mistake their lust for a more potent feeling while also pushing them to impress you just to get closer to achieving their target, which is having you. The key is in the timing. You have to be able to realize when the target might be losing interest and also recognize the steps you have to take to reignite their interest. Finally, you have to know when to give in. It would be better for your ploy if you have the sexual prowess to match your games as this would make you less of a pretender and more of the real deal.

If properly played, a game of seductive manipulation could lead to real feelings and would thus make the target even more dependent on you. Everyone is susceptible to this sort of manipulation because we all crave emotional and physical relationships with others regardless of how small the urge is.

HOW TO PROPERLY MANIPULATE STRANGERS

Strangers are the hardest to manipulate or persuade because you usually have no idea how they think, how they process information or what makes them tick. In fact, most of the time, when you approach a stranger you find yourself following your instincts and searching for a foothold in their minds that you can leverage into a real connection. This is the smart way to go when dealing with individuals you barely know but such a method is slow and could end up being frustrating.

The alternative is quicker, riskier and used mostly by pick up artists. It is one in which you walk up to the target and impress he or she with an intoxicating mix of charm, wit and the promise of a very interesting future. This plan could fall by the wayside if your version of humor doesn't click with theirs or if your target is in the wrong state of mind for your ploy to have an effect.

Another way is to go all out and state what you want. This is rarely utilized, mostly because it betrays the very essence of manipulation; secrecy and emotional control. It is also rarely successful, so unless you are feeling lucky or the universe seems to be in your corner, don't try it.

CHAPTER 10

MANIPULATING AND SCOUTING: THE FORGOTTEN CONNECTION

I like to compare the game of manipulation to the hunting rituals of a predator while hunting a prey. When hunting prey, the lions of the African savannah watch their unfortunate prey - say a herd of wildebeests grazing in the distance. The lions (usually a pride) lie in wait, studying the unsuspecting prey, analyzing the herd and seeking out the weak and the vulnerable of the herd, pretty much scouting the herd. After successfully picking a target, the lions then plan a mode of attack, assigning the roles of distraction and decoys to certain individuals of the pack, some to cut off the escape routes of the prey and finally one or more to finally bring down the prey.

The manipulation game isn't too different from the scenario explained above. When scouting, the idea is not to hide or to skulk in the dark but rather to size up your target emotionally and psychologically. It is the process by which you identify the initial footholds present in their minds and how they could be used to your advantage.

Naturally, when starting the process of manipulation with a stranger, you are usually starting out blind but when you skip the scouting phase altogether, you consign yourself to starting out on the weakest possible footing, further reducing your chances of succeeding.

WATCHING YOUR TARGET IS IMPORTANT

This is the first step and the very foundation of manipulating a target. As shown by the hunting lions, watching or studying gives you a basic info of the target helping you understand the targets habits, likes and dislikes, wants and aspirations of such target that can be exploited. Things that would prove useful in your arsenal for securing the target. A knowledge of the relevant basic info of a target reveals the weak points of such target, providing spots to be exploited to get what is needed and knowing how to trigger such target to get the required result. A good example of those weak points is the human emotions.

As humans, a considerable amount of us tend to act and make decisions under the influence of our emotions and are as a result, slaves to our emotions. Emotions make a man because they are his basest, truest reactions to a situation and most of the time we fall victim to our own emotions, expressing them without control and as such leaving us exposed to the ministrations and knowledgeable tweaking of manipulators. As earlier implied, you must always reserve extreme control over your own emotions and judge every situation logically. This helps you make the right decisions in every situation and also protects you from manipulation as you are the only one with a knowledge of your feelings.

These emotions can act as catalysts to the decision-making process of the human mind without a lot of us realizing it. For example, an altruistic person - that selfless individual who wants to do right by everyone. Such person's need to satisfy everyone can be exploited by the classic guilt trip move, by making them feel sad and unfulfilled and making them do what you want.

The knowledge gleaned from watching a target cannot be underestimated and should be of immense importance to your initial actions concerning such a target, guiding your action and words.

ESTABLISHING TRUST

The importance of trust in manipulation can never be overstated. It is like the key which finally opens a door to a lost store of gems and treasures. just like without the key, you have no access to the treasures which lay inside, so can you not truly manipulate a person without gaining their trust. This is the mistake made by pseudo manipulators and you would do well not to make similar ones. They make the mistake of misjudging how much the target trusts them and as such show their hand too early. As a result, they are exposed to manipulation themselves because they then trust every one of your actions and words to be as a result of their influence.

Trust has always been an active and essential ingredient for a successful human relationship. A child trusts its parent(s) that is why he/she can follow such parent to anywhere without fear for harm. So, it is with is with the targets of manipulation, once you have secured their trust, you become infallible, your decisions are regarded to be the accurate, and your word is held in highest regard.

In some cases, this trust is easily gotten, like in the instance of the altruistic, good-willing and generally naive people. But in other cases, it is not always gotten so easily as one might have to go through various tests to finally earn that trust, but once the trust is finally earned, it is always worth the effort.

You basically have them in the palm of your hand at this level, and they are as clay in the hands of a potter in your own hands - ready to bend to whatever direction you may wish.

The subject of trust is also a critical one as trust is as easy to lose as it is hard to gain. A couple of mistakes could easily cause you to lose the hard-earned trust of a target, and trust when lost, isn't always exactly gotten back. Even if it is gotten back, it is never always in full.

PLANNING A STRATEGY OF APPROACH

Most of the time, for any endeavor to be successful you need a strategy. Referencing the predator/prey scenario earlier stated, a strategy is a means towards an end or ultimate result. The word strategy brings the game of chess to mind. Every smart player knows that to win, a strategy must be in place to achieve such result. If trust is the key to a den of treasures, then your strategy is your plan to avoid the uncanny traps placed around to prevent seekers from reaching the treasure. The manipulation of a target has now become like a game of chess where your every move must be tailored and aimed to getting what you want. It has become a game which for every action of the target, there should be a suitable reaction on the part of the manipulator to help get what is needed.

Since human beings can be quite dissimilar in terms of constitution, intelligence and emotional make-up, it goes without saying that one strategy cannot work for all and different strategies should be employed for different targets and different occasions. One can choose to work a target little by little, slowly but surely getting the required result or one could alternatively leave a "bait" for the target and wait patiently for the bite.

The strategy applied must take into consideration the default emotional state of the target, the level of isolation of the target, the peculiarities of the person as well as the general nature of the person. All of this are very important and neglect of anyone could lead to failure.

FOLLOW ONLY WHAT YOU SEE OR HEAR

This is in a way related to the first point. Watching and studying the target would provide you with clues to exploit when working a target. These clues should be your pointers, guiding you on the next step to take or what to say next. But contrary to the first point, this is a warning. You should never try to use a clue or a feeling not present in a particular target against him/her.

As humans, we possess the tendency to judge people based on what we would do in their shoes and not based on what they have shown they would do. You have to kick out this tendency as it could mess with your reactions to the targets actions even without clouding your judgement. It makes you doubt the soundness of your judgement, pushing you to react against what you would do and feel instead of what you can observe the target doing or feeling.

Indiscriminate or excessive use of such could put you in trouble and you could ruin the whole process, causing you to start the whole process all the way from the beginning. Never forget, the idea behind a successful manipulation is determining the targets emotional state and reactions and using this to your advantage. Never let doubt creep in and spoil what is already almost done, only follow what you can see and hear and nothing else.

CONCLUSION

Understanding the key to manipulation and persuasion is very useful in daily human life. Each facet and form requires its own special skillset to really bring them to life and I hope this book has shown you enough in terms of how to achieve that.

When you understand how to effectively persuade people to your mode of reasoning and manipulate them without their knowledge, you are bound to get more out of situations regardless of whether they are business or relationship scenarios. Eventually, being able to manipulate people to your advantage would increase your influence in life and this influence would bring you success.

Good luck in using the skills you have learned from this book and I hope you experience as much joy in learning as I enjoyed in making this book.

A final word of advice, never give up easily; nothing good ever comes easy and practice makes perfect.

Lastly, if you enjoyed this book I ask that you please take the time to review it on Audible.com. Your honest feedback would be greatly appreciated.

Thank you.

Now, I would like to share with you a free sneak peek to another one of my books that I think you will really enjoy.

The book is called "Manipulation Techniques to Influence People: Dark Psychology 202" Published by Sebastian Cooper and Brandon Goff. It's A Practical Guide to Learn Persuasion Methods, Analyze People, Mind Control 101, Dark NLP, Dark CBT, Deception and Brainwashing Hypnotism.

Enjoy!

Chapter 1: Introduction to Dark Psychology

It's a bit of a well-kept secret that the ability to manipulate people is a useful tool. It's one of the reasons how businessmen and politicians get and hold their positions. There comes a certain point in your life wherein completely turning off your emotions and being pragmatic is a skill you need to have. Nobody likes to discuss it because we have this societal fear of the reality that people can just be seen as a means to an end.

The late Steve Jobs was particularly renowned for his ability to work people's emotions and to say just the right thing that would get them to come around to his view. It was so strong, in fact, that the people around him developed their own term for it: the 'reality distortion field,' a phrase coined from a similar phenomenon in the Star Trek universe.

There are numerous historical instances of Steve Jobs taking advantage of his unique ability to get precisely what he wanted. One such instance was when Jobs, in the 1980s, was trying to get Pepsi CEO John Sculley to come to Apple. This exchange spawned a famous line that many know today: "Do you want to sell sugared water for the rest of your life, or do you want to come with me and change the world?"

There is a lot that can be said about his specific ability to charm and manipulate people, not the least of which was his deep understanding of what people wanted as well as what people wanted to hear. Add on to this an understanding of subtle intimidation, power cues, and a large amount of passion and charisma, and you have a powerhouse who could get pretty much whatever he wanted.

How does all of this apply to you? Well, you're reading this because you want to learn how to work with people from the inside out. You want to know how to say just the right thing to get what you need and how to manipulate people such that you can bypass any obstacles, so they will do exactly what you want. If that's the case, then you've come to the right place.

The fact is that the mind is a relatively simple thing. While the brain is infinitely complex, the manifestations of the conscious mind are both resolute and easy to work with. Most people work in very obvious and predictable ways such that if they're a 'normal' person, you can rather easily figure out the best way to work with them in no time flat.

The purpose is to analyze all of these patterns within the context of people in general so that you can learn the best way to put these trends to use. Some people will, of course, break these 'standard' molds, and for this reason there are a couple chapters dedicated to the idea of knowing the person you're working with, reading their inner and outer body language and mental cues, and knowing how to build a paradigm that you can easily manipulate them with.

In the end, this is about using the concept of neuro-linguistic programming to its fullest to get what you want out of people. A more common term for this is 'manipulation.' However, the aim of neuro-linguistic programming is slightly different. Neuro-linguistic programming is more focused on the long-term shifting of attitudes where manipulation is more based on immediate gains. That isn't to say that neuro-linguistic programming isn't a form of manipulation though, it absolutely is.

When you hear the term 'manipulation,' you will probably have some sort of knee-jerk reaction like, "Wait, isn't manipulation wrong?" And to this question, there is no simple answer.

I have to say no, though. Manipulation isn't wrong, manipulation is simply a tool. How you use it can determine whether it's wrong or not. For example, an example of manipulation being objectively wrong is doing something that gets somebody terribly hurt. There are also some unspoken rules that you should never break. For example, while it's pretty easy to take advantage of the fact that somebody's parent is dying, actually doing so is a major ethical gray area.

If you stick to maintaining an ethical approach, then manipulation actually proves itself as a method of understanding people and knowing how to work with them so things will work out better for you. You can even use manipulation for good purposes. One such example is Steve Jobs yet again, who used his reality distortion field for good causes, such as when he would convince his employees that it was possible to do something that was more or less impossible, which in turn, would make them work harder for the end result and eventually lead to a new mark being set in technology.

We all know that psychology is the study and analysis of the human mind and human behavior. So, what is Dark Psychology? It is the science and art of manipulating and controlling the human mind through various methods. Psychology is central to human interactions, thoughts, and actions whereas Dark Psychology involves the use of tactics of persuasion, motivation, coercion, and manipulation to get what you want.

There is a phenomenon in this realm referred to as the Dark Psychology Triad that consists of elements that help in detecting potential criminal behavior in people. The Dark Triad is a combination of traits including Narcissism, Machiavellianism, and Psychopathy. What are the characteristic features of each of these Dark Triad traits?

- Narcissism – is related to lack of empathy, high levels of egotism, and grandiosity

- Machiavellianism – People with this attitude have little or no sense of morality and ruthlessly employ manipulation and other tactics to exploit and/or deceive others.

- Psychopathy – These people come across as very charming and charismatic and deep down are highly impulsive, selfish, lack empathy, and are fairly remorseless.

Yes, it is true that none of us wants to be manipulated and yet it happens in our daily lives with unerring regularity, many times unwittingly. Additionally, we also use mind control and manipulation tactics to try and get what we want. Dark Psychology involves studying the psychodynamics of people who prey on and victimize others to achieve their own ends.

There are people who use dark psychology tactics knowingly and with the intention to cause harm to others and there are those who use or are prey to these tactics in unwitting ways. Moreover, it is a survival instinct in all living beings to be wary of our surroundings and use guile and deception to survive and thrive. There are multiple studies that prove this innate ability to victimize others.

Although we believe that we have control over our actions and reactions, under extreme pressure, it is very difficult to predict our behaviors and there are high chances that many employ dark tactics to escape from these pressures. The following studies are examples of how human minds behave in unpredictable ways when compelled or sometimes even when it may not have needed such an extreme reaction.

Let us look at some of these experiments conducted in the '60s and '70s by psychologists. While there are controversies surrounding the experiments and plausible rationalizations were provided in retrospect, it goes without doubt that the human mind can be very unpredictable and is capable of reaching out to its dark aspects with little or no provocation.

The 'learner' was actually only an actor.

If the learner gave a wrong answer, the volunteers were told to give electric shocks by turning the 'dial', which had labels ranging from mild pain to extreme pain to even fatal. The experimenter wearing a lab coat told the volunteers that they should continue to increase the intensity of the 'electric shock' until the right answer was given by the learner. The volunteers could hear the simulated screams of the learner from the other room. If the volunteer did not want to increase the intensity, then the experiment told them to continue employing the following statements:

- Please continue
- The experiment needs you to go on
- It is essential that you go on
- You have no choice; you have to go on

There were startling and disturbing outcomes from this rather controversial experiment. Despite hearing the simulated screams of extreme pain from the 'learners,' 65% of the volunteers turned the knob to 'fatal.' They did not even bother to ask about the health of the learner. Yet, most of the volunteers said that they would have never behaved this way but did not find the wherewithal to stand up to a figure of authority (lab-coated experimenter). Dark Psychology is easy to trigger, isn't it?

The most disturbing observation of these kinds of experiments was the fact that the volunteers were not even aware that they were being manipulated and that they were delving into the dark aspects of their minds. Another study which proved the unconscious behavior under authority goes as follows:

A group of volunteers was asked to watch a screen in which a basketball game was going on. They were told to count the number of passes that took place between players wearing white shirts. At some point during the game, a person dressed in a gorilla costume walked into the court. The participants were so engrossed in counting the number of passes that they did not even notice this aberration. In fact, many participants swore that no such disturbance took place! They were unconsciously following the orders of the experimenter.

Another common dark psychology tactic is called 'priming' in which people's behaviors can be changed without them even realizing it. For example, read this sentence, 'The house was so old that it groaned, creaked, and struggled to stand on its shaky foundation.' Now, suppose you were to stand up, chances are very high that you will unconsciously have taken care to do so at a slower pace than usual as you were just now 'primed' for old age.

Politicians are known to use priming to change voting preferences based on the location of the booth. Like this, there are many studies which prove that accessing and employing the dark side of our minds is not just easy but can happen without us even being aware of it.

Moreover, these theories have been applied and checked repeatedly throughout the history of mankind and dark psychology is an integral part of our minds. This is not the same as conspiracy theories. Dark psychology only represents the innate need and desire for man to dominate over others who are weaker than himself so as to achieve his own ends. Marketing advertisements are classic examples of manipulating the minds of the buyers and convincing them to buy the product, which they may or may not need.

Therefore, it makes sense to know, understand, and appreciate this aspect of our minds and use strategies and tips to 'prime' our minds and those of others in ways that will result in win-win situations for all concerned stakeholders.

Persuasion

Persuasion is one of the most popular forms of mind control. This method is used in so many different areas of life that many people don't even recognize when it is happening. That is exactly why it works.

Persuasion is not the same as convincing, although most people believe the two are the same thing. However, persuasion is the act of skillfully encouraging someone to do what you want them to do without them realizing you're doing it, whereas convincing someone means that you are using tactics that are easy to recognize. To explain it a bit further, persuading means to skillfully present facts and information in a way that doesn't make it obvious that you are doing so, and encouraging people to do what you desire for them to do. Convincing people, on the other hand, is very obvious and often includes a lot of back-and-forth and ultimately nagging, begging, or pleading someone to make the decision you want them to make after they have already chosen the alternative.

When you are learning about persuasion, it may seem easy. In reality, it is a strategy that requires a lot of time, effort, and practice. You cannot simply read about persuasion and then run out and master it. Instead, you really need to ensure that you grasp the concept and that you practice putting it into action in your daily life. In chapter 6 you will learn about many real-life strategies that can help you further integrate this technique into your life.

Manipulation

Manipulation tends to be regarded as one of the darker methods of mind control, and many people think it is a nasty thing to do. However, when you learn to use manipulation properly, you can use it to gain control over virtually anyone's mind and have your desired effect on their decisions and actions.

Unlike persuasion, which is typically comprised of conversational tactics, manipulation involves external influences to help encourage people to do what you want them to do. These include strategies like building trust, and proving why they should do what you want them to do. While some of these strategies are conversational, they are often impacted by external influences unlike persuasion which relies merely on wording structure and methods of structuring your sentences and conversations.

Deception

Deception is an extremely sophisticated strategy that is used in mind control. This is not the process of outright lying to people, but rather tactfully covering up certain pieces of information to avoid them from ever being discovered. This strategy allows people to knowingly omit information from conversations without being considered liars since they have never directly been asked, and therefore they have never directly lied.

When you are partaking in deception, you have to be tactful and consistent in keeping the conversation away from any question that may put you in a position where you must either come clean or actually lie. Using deception as a secondary manipulation method for mind control purposes means controlling the conversation and preventing it from ever going in the direction that would suggest information that you are lying or covering up information.

In order to skillfully use deception, you need to know how to guide the conversation in a way that leads the listener to believe something without ever actually being told to believe it. For example, if you want to prevent someone from finding out that you are attracted to someone they also like, you could create the illusion that you are not. You never actually admit that you aren't, you just lead the conversation so that it can be assumed that you aren't.

This is a powerful form of mind control because it allows you to deny ever doing anything wrong. Since you have never admitted to anything or lied about anything, you can easily say that it was the listeners fault for not asking, or for assuming anything was implied.

Subliminal Messages

When you use subliminal messages, you are sending messages without someone actually knowing that you are doing so. These messages tend to slip past the conscious mind and directly into the subconscious. The powerful thing about subliminal messages is that you can be telling someone one thing, and yet having them hear something entirely different. While this conscious mind digests something that they are willingly accepting, their subconscious mind may be hearing something entirely different. Because you have put them into a receptive mode, they are more likely to react and respond in the way that you want them to, and their subconscious mind is more likely to accept the information as well.

Subliminal messaging is powerful because it allows you to control the mind without any indication that you are doing so. You can speak directly through the conscious mind and into the subconscious mind, thus planting information, evidence, and knowledge into the subconscious that encourages your listener to support your position and act or think in the way that you want them to. You are literally programming their mind with your desired messages, and they have no idea that you are doing so.

Mind control is a very powerful strategy that can enable you to have people thinking in your favor. These individuals are going to unknowingly be listening extremely closely to your sentences and hanging on your every word, while giving into anything you want. Because of your masterful ability to control their minds without them even knowing it, you will be able to have any desired outcome effortlessly.

People often have a few different traits which you can use to understand them. Things such as their body language, their life situation, and their emotions. All of these impact one another. In the following chapters, we will break down all of these aspects to help you understand exactly what position you're in.

Body language is a huge giveaway about what's going on in a person's head. Understand that in terms of neuro-linguistic programming, body language is a language in and of itself.

We're going to expand on this concept just a bit so we can gain an understanding of how we can read and process other people's emotions.

This is actually a very critical part of neuro-linguistic programming, and one of the things that makes it such a challenge. Doing it properly is not like picking a lock. There is no 'correct' path for you to do it right. It's a very dynamic activity, which is heavily centered on your ability to understand what the other person is thinking in a very concrete manner.

Understand that a person has many physical tells, but that's not the be-all-end-all of what is going on in a person's mind. Some people are so good at hiding their emotions that you can't really tell what's going on under the hood unless you know them very well.

Often, people will have two emotions running in parallel. These can be difficult to decipher, but generally, they have the emotion at their foreground — this is what they display themselves to be feeling — and they have their emotion in the background, which is what they are feeling under the hood.

Some people are worse than others when it comes to hiding their emotions while some people make no effort at all. There are times, too, where these emotions may run in tandem and are exactly the same.

The truth is, though, that if you're trying to convince somebody of something, you always have to consider the possibility that people don't often feel what they're projecting themselves to be feeling. Usually, you have to consider what these parallel emotions could be.

We'll focus more on the underlying emotions when we get to the chapter on psychoanalysis. However, for now, we just need to focus primarily on reading emotions on the surface.

People convey a lot of their emotions through their body language as well as through their tone of voice and their choice of words.

If you pay attention to a person's eyes, you can read a lot into somebody's foreground emotion. While, hopefully, you're emotionally competent enough to read foreground emotions relatively well, note that some of these can be difficult to break apart from one another. For example, while the difference between annoyance and anger are slight in terms of their physical display, they have far different emotional connotations. Annoyance is much shorter and less severe, though perhaps more immediately snappy. Anger is more brooding and harder to work your way out of.

Their tone of voice will also tell you a lot. Often, when people aren't being completely honest about the emotion they're presenting, their voice will sound ever so slightly off. Being able to recognize this and using context clues to figure out what's really bothering them or going on in their head is very important.

Sometimes their choice of words will give you hints as well. Pay attention and try to notice if their sentences are structured differently. Are they shorter? Is their choice of words more serious than usual?

In essence, pay attention to a person's body language, as it will tell you a lot about what you need to know when it comes to what a person is feeling, at least on the surface level. When you combine that with your analysis of their underlying conditions, you actually get a very potent piece of information that you can work with.

NLP – Neuro-Linguistic Programming

NLP involves the three most powerful elements that contribute to the human experience and they are; neurology, language, and programming. So, how can we use NLP to influence people? Here are some answers to that.

NLP techniques are in use both in businesses and personal relationships to influence people around you. NLP techniques are designed to help you get your message across in the correct way so that they are interpreted by the people to give you your desired outcomes. NLP techniques also focus on the choice and appropriate use of language to help you motivate people around you to get something good done.

NLP techniques are designed in such a way that if used correctly, they can help you teach others how to become more productive and efficient in their lives which, in turn, helps you in your life as well. NLP techniques are also designed for salespeople so that they are able to reach the subconscious levels of the buyers' minds in such a way that they feel good and happy about buying the product or service.

The basic presumption of NLP is that each of us is unique in the way we think, we interpret, and the way we present ourselves to the outside world. NLP says that if we know how we think, then we can be empowered to change the way we think. Extending the same logic outside of us, if we know how people think, we can empower ourselves and them to influence changes in their thought processes.

Let us take an example. Each of us has a unique way of translating what we see around us into thoughts. Our preference could be to the use of sight, sound or touch or a unique combination of all three. If our preferred sense is that of sight, then we easily convert the events in our life into pictures and images in our thoughts. If our preferred sense is that of touch, we easily convert our experiences into feelings.

Let's take this a bit further. Suppose you had a preference for the sense of sight. This preferred sense is actually very evident in the way you interact with others. For example, you will use phrases like, 'See you later,' or 'I can see how this will turn out,' etc. You will normally be the type of person who decides that when something or someone is out of sight, then that person or thing is out of your mind too.

So, with a person whose sense preference is that of touch, phrases such as 'Catch you later,' or 'I'm getting a bad feeling from this,' etc. will be used. So, by knowing these preferences and the way they become evident through their language and thought, we can understand people better and once we understand their behavior, we can more easily influence the way they think.

It is a natural thing to be fond of those individuals who are like us in the way they think and behave. So, by knowing their preferred means of communication, we can use the same way to communicate with them and therefore make it easy for us to influence them.

A classic example of NLP influencing technique is to synchronize your breathing with that of the other person. Watch when the person breathes in and you match your inhalation with that. When you match every breath of yours with the other person's, you will find an invisible connection to the individual giving you a great boost in terms of influencing his or her thoughts.

Thank you, this preview is now over.

I hope you enjoyed this preview of my book "Dark Psychology: Proven Manipulation Techniques to Influence Human Psychology" Published by John Clark. Please make sure to check out the full book on Amazon.com

Thank you.

BOOST YOUR CONFIDENCE & SELF-ESTEEM WITH INSPIRING AFFIRMATIONS

Radically Increase Your Self-Awareness in Just 7 Days with Incredible Motivational Affirmations and Positive Quotes

TABLE OF CONTENTS

- LOW SELF-ESTEEM AND QUALITY OF LIFE 96
- CAUSES OF LOW SELF-ESTEEM 97
- HOW TO MAKE THE POWER OF AFFIRMATIONS WORK FOR YOU EVERYDAY? 98
- AFFIRMATIONS FOR SELF-ESTEEM AND CONFIDENCE 101
- QUOTES FOR SELF-ESTEEM 158
- SELF-ESTEEM HYPNOSIS 166
- HYPNOSIS FOR CONFIDENCE.. 167
- SELF-WORTH VISUALIZATION SCRIPT 171
- SELF-CONFIDENCE HYPNOSIS SCRIPT............................178
- SELF-CONFIDENCE HYPNOSIS.. 181
- THIS SESSION IS OVER; WE WILL NOW KEEP GOING WITH THE NEXT SESSION. 182
- SELF-ESTEEM HYPNOSIS 182
- FOR OUR LAST SESSION WE WILL BE DOING SELF-ESTEEM HYPNOSIS. PREPARE YOURSELVES AS WE WILL BE STARTING THE SESSION, TO BEGIN: ...183

Congratulations on purchasing Motivational Affirmations to Boost Confidence and Self-Esteem - The Most Powerful Subliminal Affirmations, Hypnosis and Quotes to Radically Increase Self-Confidence and Recognize Your Self-Worth book and thank you for doing so!

This book will be all about the best affirmations and quotes to motivate you and boost your self-esteem which will give you the confidence needed in your day to day life. This will help you especially if you are experiencing hardships and shortcomings. We will go over the different affirmations and quotes that are carefully chosen to overcome your challenges whatever they are. The content in this book will guide you along the way and help you to attain a spectacular amount of self-esteem.

Thanks again for choosing us. Every effort was made to ensure it is full of as much useful content as possible. Please enjoy!

LOW SELF-ESTEEM AND QUALITY OF LIFE

A low self-esteem can reduce the quality of a person's life in many different ways, including:

•	Negative feelings – the constant self-criticism can lead to persistent feelings of sadness, depression, anxiety, anger, shame or guilt.

•	Relationship problems – for example they may tolerate all sorts of unreasonable behaviour from partners because they believe they must earn love and friendship, cannot be loved or are not loveable. Alternatively, a person with low self-esteem may feel angry and bully other people.

•	Fear of trying – the person may doubt their abilities or worth and avoid challenges.

•	Perfectionism – a person may push themselves and become an over-achiever to 'atone' for what they see as their inferiority.

•	Fear of judgment – they may avoid activities that involve other people, like sports or social events, because they are afraid they will be negatively judged. The person feels self-conscious and stressed around others and constantly looks for 'signs' that people don't like them.

•	Low resilience – a person with low self-esteem finds it hard to cope with a challenging life event because they already believe themselves to be 'hopeless'.

•	Lack of self-care – the person may care so little that they neglect or abuse themselves, for example, drink too much alcohol.

•	Self-harming behaviours – low self-esteem puts the person at increased risk of self-harm, for example, eating disorder, drug abuse or suicide.

CAUSES OF LOW SELF-ESTEEM

Some of the many causes of low self-esteem may include:

- Unhappy childhood where parents (or other significant people such as teachers) were extremely critical

- Poor academic performance in school resulting in a lack of confidence

- Ongoing stressful life event such as relationship breakdown or financial trouble

- Poor treatment from a partner, parent or career, for example, being in an abusive relationship

- Ongoing medical problem such as chronic pain, serious illness or physical disability

- Mental illness such as an anxiety disorder or depression.

HOW TO MAKE THE POWER OF AFFIRMATIONS WORK FOR YOU EVERYDAY?

As you sit there reading this, I'm sure you realize you need to use affirmations daily to make the change that you need in your life...the idea behind this is to change your focus to a positive one. This will not happen instantly but requires repeated effort over time. So please don't give up on this if it doesn't seem to help immediately.

I suggest you repeat affirmations at least twice a day during the morning and evening when you get time. At first you may not feel like you agree with some of the things you are saying but eventually you will change the way you think and act and that is the purpose of these statements. Try putting some of your emotions into the words and they will become so much more powerful.

Self affirmation is so important if you want to build your self esteem because you need to keep telling yourself positive things – the results will be immense because there is no greater criticism that we face than that which we give ourselves. Having a positive outlook is like putting on armor or carrying weapons that will protect you in your daily life.

Using positive affirmations to manifest change in your life is a great way to boost self-esteem. I normally place sticky notes in my bathroom mirror filled with positive affirmations, so it can be the first thing I see in the morning. I hope you have enjoyed these self esteem affirmations

Tips in Building Confidence and Self-Esteem

1. Make two lists: one of your strengths and one of your achievements. Try to get a supportive friend or relative to help you with these lists, as people with low self-esteem are not usually in the most objective frame of mind. Keep the lists in a safe place and read through them every morning.

2. Think positively about yourself. Remind yourself that, despite your problems, you are a unique, special, and valuable person, and that you deserve to feel good about yourself. You are, after all, a miracle of consciousness, the consciousness of the universe. Identify and challenge any negative thoughts about yourself such as 'I am loser', 'I never do anything right', or 'No one really likes me'.

3. Pay special attention to your personal hygiene: take a shower, brush your hair, trim your nails, and so on.

4. Wear clean clothes that make you feel good about yourself. All things being equal, wear an ironed shirt rather than a crumpled T-shirt, you get the idea.

5. Eat good food as part of a healthy, balanced diet. Make meals a special time, even if you are eating alone. Turn off the TV, set the table, light a candle, and make a moment to feel grateful.

6. Exercise regularly. Go for a brisk walk every day, even if it is cold or rainy, and take more vigorous exercise (exercise that makes you sweat) three times a week.

7. Ensure that you're getting enough sleep. See my article Better Sleep in 10 Simple Steps.

8. Reduce your stress levels. If possible, agree with a friend or relative that you will take turns to massage each other on a regular basis. For other suggestions, see my article Managing Stress.

9. Make your living space clean, comfortable, and attractive. Whenever I clean my windows or just water my plants I seem to feel much better. Display items that remind you of your achievements and the special times and people in your life.

10. Do more of the things that you enjoy. Go ahead and spoil yourself. Do at least one thing that you enjoy every day.

11. Get artistic. Activities like painting, music, poetry, and dance enable you to express yourself, interact positively with others, and reduce your stress levels. You might even impress yourself! Find a

class through your local adult education service or community center.

12. Set yourself a challenge that you can realistically complete. For example, take up yoga, learn to sing, or throw a small dinner party for some friends. Just go for it!

13. Do some of the things that you have been putting off, such as filing the paperwork, repainting the kitchen, or clearing out the garden.

14. Be nice to people, and do nice things for them. For instance, strike up a conversation with the postman or shopkeeper, invite a neighbor round for tea, visit a friend who is sick, or get involved with a local charity. Putting a smile on someone's face is bound to put one on yours.

15. Get others on board. Tell your friends and relatives what you are going through and ask for their advice and support. Perhaps they too have similar problems, in which case you might be able to band together and form a support group. Don't be overly shy or reserved: most people do want to help!

16. Spend more time with those you hold near and dear. At the same time, try to enlarge your social circle by making an effort to meet and befriend people.

17. Avoid people and places that treat you badly or make you feel bad about yourself. This could mean being more assertive. If assertiveness is a problem for you, ask a health professional about assertiveness training.

AFFIRMATIONS FOR SELF-ESTEEM AND CONFIDENCE

Get yourselves ready and listen carefully as we will start the affirmation session:

- I have the strength of mind to make difficult choices that will benefit me.
- I have survived 100% of my toughest days and I will survive whatever comes next.
- I know that the universe has my back & will give me what I need to become stronger.
- I am in the process of becoming my strongest version – mentally, physically, emotionally and spiritually.
- There is nothing standing in my way, every obstacle I see is an opportunity for growth.
- I choose to let my past make me better and not bitter.
- I love and accept myself exactly as I am today.
- I acknowledge how blessed I am to be alive today.
- I choose to see each new day as an opportunity to experience life.
- I know that fear is false evidence
- I won't give up when times get hard and things stop being easy.
- I'm done being used and taken advantage of.
- What I say about myself is more important than what other people say about me.
- If I make a promise to myself I'm going to keep it. Confidence comes from trust. If I can trust myself I can be more confident.
- I have my entire future to think about. I can't mess this up over some foolishness.
- I am the architect of my life; I build its foundation and choose its contents.
- Today, I am brimming with energy and overflowing with joy.

- My body is healthy; my mind is brilliant; my soul is tranquil.
- I am superior to negative thoughts and low actions.
- I have been given endless talents which I begin to utilize today.
- I've hated my body for years so I deserve to feel confident and love every bit of it now.
- I'm going to focus my mind on bettering myself instead of concentrating on negativity.
- I'm comfortable with who I am, I'm confident in where I'm going I don't need to play the comparison game.
- I'm not going to allow my fear of loneliness forces me into bad friendships with people who aren't good for me.
- I'm done being used and taken advantage of.
- I won't give up when times get hard and things stop being easy.
- What I say about myself is more important than what other people say about me.
- If I make a promise to myself I'm going to keep it. Confidence comes from trust. If I can trust myself I can be more confident.
- I used to walk into a room full of people and wonder if they liked me… now I look around and wonder if I like them.
- I am in the process of becoming the happiest and most confident version of myself.
- My confidence isn't built off compliments. It's built on mastery and competence.
- I value my worth. I am talented. I'm not going to sell myself short.
- I am a worthwhile and lovable person.
- I believe I can do more than others say I can.
- When I breathe, I inhale confidence and exhale timidity.
- I love meeting strangers and approach them with boldness and enthusiasm.
- I approve of myself and love myself deeply and completely.
- I live in the present and am confident of the future.
- My personality exudes confidence. I am bold and outgoing,

- Self-confidence is what I thrive on. Nothing is impossible and life is great.
- I always see only the good in others. I attract only positive people.
- I face difficult situations with courage and conviction. I always find a way out of such situations.
- I am doing the best I can with the knowledge and experience I have obtained so far.
- It's OK to make mistakes. They are opportunities to learn.
- I always follow through on my promises.
- I treat others with kindness and respect.
- I see myself with kind eyes.
- I am a unique and a very special person.
- I love myself more each day.
- I am willing to change.
- I am unique; I feel great about being alive and being me.
- Amazing opportunities exist for me in every aspect of my life.
- Challenges bring out the best in me, so naturally, I love them.
- I create positive & supportive relationships.
- I trust myself.
- Each day I am becoming more self-confident.
- I appreciate all that I do.
- I can't live my life waiting for other people to approve of who I am. I have to love who I am and who I am becoming.
- I'm done letting folks getting under my skin. I'm going to stay focused on things that really matter.
- I believe I can accomplish the goals I'm setting for myself. I'm being honest about what I want and I know why I need to accomplish these goals.
- Impressing people isn't that important. I like who I am.
- My past may be ugly, but I am still beautiful.
- I am worthy of becoming successful with what I love doing.
- I have enough knowledge to be successful in the field of my choice.
- I have enough knowledge to help many people on their path.

- I have what it takes to succeed.
- I am great at what I do and my success is inevitable.
- There are going to be haters everywhere I just have to stay grounded and focused.
- I'm not going to let anyone write me off. I respect my worth.
- I have to learn to speak up for myself.
- I can still be respectful but I have to let people know that they can't walk all over me.
- I will defend myself if I have too. I won't let people walk all over me.
- I will make and keep promises to myself. I will regain trust in myself. I will repair my confidence.
- I am my best friend. Others may come and go, but I am always here for me.
- I am enough on my own. I do not need others to validate me,
- I fully accept myself and know that I am worthy of great things in life.
- I find deep inner peace within myself as I am.
- My mind is wide open to all the possibilities around me
- I am abundant in all areas of my life
- What I think about I bring about, therefore I only think about what I desire
- Success comes easily to me
- I have rock solid belief in myself and my ability to succeed
- My mind has no resistance to abundance and new opportunity
- Everyone around me believes in me and my success
- My nature is success and abundance
- I see prosperity wherever I kook
- Whatever I can envision, It will become so
- I manage my time like a successful person
- I believe in myself and know I have what it takes to succeed
- I grow everyday to ensure my success
- I am the essence of success
- I will be the most successful in my chosen field

- I have what it takes to succeed
- Success is seeking me
- I only think in abundant ways
- I notice new income opportunities all around me
- I only allow abundant beliefs to operate in me
- I attract prosperity in my life with ease
- I am always open to new financial endeavors and streams of income
- I receive money with ease
- I create active and passive forms of income with ease
- Money comes to me from unexpected sources
- The entire universe is aspiring to make me successful
- I live in a mindset of prosperity
- I am a success magnet
- My vision of success carries me through any hard time
- I am appreciated for the value I bring
- I have all the money I need
- I am excited about being a success in all areas of my life
- Success feels great
- I create solutions to my problems with ease
- I have encouraging and successful friends
- I gain confidence daily
- I live out my full potential daily
- I always find myself in the best of the best circumstances
- My success allows me to contribute massively to the betterment of mankind
- My high standards are always matched with my fantastic work ethic
- My dreams and ambitions have no limits
- I always feel grateful for my success
- Every time a negative habits comes into my mind, I let it go automatically
- I always have more than enough
- I face my fears, allowing me to become more powerful and creating even more self belief

- My power is unlimited
- My intuition guides me to success
- My motivation is always very high
- I work under pressure with ease
- Calmness and confidence emanate through my being
- My self confidence builds upon itself daily
- I am free to express my passions and get highly paid for them
- I am the creator of my own universe
- People notice how I am naturally successful
- I have the Midas touch
- I always have great ideas that can become profitable for me
- My success is acknowledged by my family and the public
- My potential and belief in myself is limitless
- I am successful in every area of my life
- I'm excited because I see my dreams manifesting daily
- Because I am committed there is always a way
- I am so grateful for the gifts I have that allow me to manifest success
- I know my mind is a powerful thing so I use it only to create a successful life for myself
- I find an ease to success in everything I do
- Money and power are seeking me
- I wake up refreshed and ready to crush my goals
- I stay ready so I don't have to get ready
- I am 100 percent in control of my life
- The power of optimism flows freely through me
- Wealth is all that surrounds me
- I don't stop until I am successful
- It is easy to achieve whatever I set out to d
- Persistence and dedication come naturally to me
- I deserve to be wealthy
- No matter what my family has done before me, I am here to change and become a success
- Success is and feels normal to me

- I have abundance in all areas of my life including money, romance and love
- I learn from my past mistakes helping me to creating a more abundant life
- I attract only the best of everything
- I am abundance
- I have faith in myself and the good that is coming to me
- I conquer challenges with ease
- I believe and can do everything my heart desires
- Positive affirmations in the morning
- I swap limiting beliefs with self empowering thoughts
- I create my destiny
- I am the master of my own fate, the captain of my own soul
- I appreciate success therefore I attract more and more of it
- Everything that happens in my life is by divine destiny
- I have infinite potential for success
- I am smart and know how to create success
- I am creating a life of abundant success
- I am proud of myself
- I attract friendships that help me create more success and love
- I persevere through anytime
- I am free from self doubt
- I was born to be successful
- I am ready for success
- I know I am becoming successful every day
- Success is how I define it
- Positive Affirmations For Women To Empower the Strong Females!
- I love my body and always will
- I am the perfect age
- I am so incredibly beautiful
- I do not let society define me and what I should look like
- I am an inspiration to others
- I workout because I love my body not because of insecurities

- I am a powerful woman
- I love taking care of my body with rest and nourishment when I need it
- I age gracefully and grow wiser each year
- My beauty lies in my heart
- My smile radiates warm motherly love
- I feel so good in my own skin
- I am always eating healthy because I love treating my body with the best
- I move at a perfect pace for myself
- I am truly equal with everyone
- I love inspiring other woman
- I love that my mate and I feel so equal in each others arms
- I enjoy having high self worth and high ideals
- I can do anything I set me mind and heart on
- I love celebrating growing older
- I love the fact that I am a woman
- I am the definition of love for my loved ones
- I care deeply and affectionately and the world appreciates me for it
- I bring to the world what no other person can
- My inner and outer beauty and love for myself grows daily
- I am doing my best and know this, that is why it is enough
- I treat myself with kindness always
- I know my gentle ways are respected and desired by all my loved ones
- I create and find power and joy from within
- I do not let my relationship status to define me
- My amazing qualities uplift everyone around me
- I am respected by my children and spouse
- My family and friends see me value and love me for me
- I love myself for who I am not who I have tried to be
- I am fearless
- I choice what I think about me, I don't define myself through other peoples opinions

- I am decisive and driven in every area of my life
- I don't have to be any body type, I love the way I look and embrace it daily
- I am an inspiration to other woman who aren't quite able to embrace their flaws
- I enjoy losing weight because I love myself and will feel great doing so
- I am a manifestation of all that is good in the world
- I live life in the now
- I reveal the good in people and search for the good in people
- I am desired because I am myself
- I am wonderful and courageous
- I am self deserving
- I am determined and diligent in the pursuit of my goals
- I know God has a perfect plan for me and I am walking in the path he has created for me
- I trust myself fully
- I purse and find peace in all relationships
- I attract positive and loving relationships into my life with ease
- I mediate on love and happiness daily
- I have so much passion and enthusiasm for life
- My life is in a constant state of progress
- I monitor my thoughts daily, replacing negative and self defeating thoughts with positive and empowering ones
- I listen to my body and what it wants
- I love the size of my breasts
- I love being present in my female cycles
- I enjoy expressing myself as a woman
- I love attracting men into my life that treat me as equal and I do the same
- I am perfect here and now
- I am open to growing in every area of my life
- Just because I don't have kids now doesn't mean I still wont find the perfect mate and be a great mother one day

- I honor my femininity
- I attract success in my career and love life
- I am a resilient woman who can adapt to anything
- I channel my female energies for the betterment of mankind
- I see myself as equal to, not better than anyone else
- I know my thoughts create my life so I only think of things that are in my hearts desires
- My soul is so beautiful
- The scares I bare are proof that you are a peaceful warrior
- Peace and happiness flow through my life like an endless river
- I am a goddess experiencing a wonderful life
- I treat all women with encouragement and support
- I only compete with myself
- I am a pure source of unconditional love
- I love the way I look, I was created to be this way
- I embrace my curves
- I am so confident in my sexuality
- Gender doesn't have to define me
- I am indestructible
- I find success with ease in everything I do in my life
- I enjoy being so prioritized and efficient in my life
- I feel a sense of high vitality and passion daily
- It is safe to be me
- My femininity is so strong
- I am assertive and respect others opinions at the same time
- I speak my mind knowing that it is OK to do so
- I am the maker of my home and that feels so powerful
- I work hard to further my career
- I am a nurturing sister and mother
- I take myself seriously but am not afraid to laugh when things don't go as planned
- Life is a series of steps and learning experiences and I grow in them daily

- I am a model mother for what my daughters will want to become and sons will seek as a mate
- I adore motherhood and feel like the ideal mother
- I love being with my soul mate and growing closer in love each day
- I heal wounds with my love and compassion
- I am a woman of substance
- I learn from my mistakes to grow daily as a strong woman
- Nothing truly defines me but my love and compassion
- Positive Affirmations For Work To Dominate Your Career!
- My boss and colleagues feel my presence of productivity and contribution
- I have my dream job
- Every situations and scenario is leading me to the perfect position that I desire
- I am recognized as an expert in my field
- A raise and promotion is in my near future
- I attract the best clients everyday
- I have so much that is special that I offer to this world
- There is nothing more special than being a mother, a sister and and aunt
- I see cold calls as warm calls
- My commissions are increasing daily
- I envision myself as a success in the workplace daily
- I have all it takes and more to excel in my field
- I separate work from my family life
- I find balance in work and rest
- I am prepared to do what it takes to be the best in my field
- I have the courage to switch careers if my current one isn't resonating with my heart
- I am a valued employee
- I enjoy growth in myself and my income through my career
- My job is a manifestation for my career vision
- I feel completely satisfied with my job and am open to growth
- I only indulge in positive habits at work that

- I am incredibly efficient at work
- I am not distracted by other employees
- I have amazing work friends
- The work I do brings benefit to society at large
- I feel a strong sense of enthusiasm at work the rubs off on my teammates
- I am sought out by colleagues for my expertise
- My positive and optimistic attitude attracts the best people to help me
- I am a masterful and professional salesperson that attracts clients in abundance
- My referral base constantly climbs as my clients feel value thorough the entire transaction and beyond
- I am a true entrepreneur as I know how to create solutions out of people's problems
- I take total ownership of everything I do at work, good and bad
- I utilize self discipline daily to reach my goals faster and faster
- I seek self-mastery within the workplace
- I get every promotion that I am ever up for
- Raises come to me out of nowhere
- I am content with my career but know I have infinite potential so stay open to other options
- I find happiness in my career but I do not seek it there
- I aim to please my customers; I turn their frown upside down
- I am a light to the work place
- I allow my passion for work drive me an enjoy financial awards because of it
- I may not be where I want to be but am working hard towards it at work and on myself
- I find and enjoy inner transformation through my work
- I create value because I am living out my passion and dreams
- I am open to other forms of wealth outside of my main job
- I do not have a ceiling on my income

- I bring uniqueness to the workplace that only I can provide
- I am the hardest worker in the room
- I feel happily content with my work when I lay down at night
- I will never limit myself in the work place
- My mind is sharp and focused each day at work
- Bad days do not effect my good days
- I am open to coaching and guidance in the work place
- I may not be where I want to work, but I am further along than yesterday
- Even when I don't feel great, I push myself because that is what winners do
- I feel like a winner in the workplace
- People know my value and show it in many ways in the workplace
- My family respects me for the work I do at my job
- I can be the boss if I want with hard enough work
- It is OK to move on from this job, it will be scary but it will be OK
- I am incredibly self sufficient at work
- I am always becoming a better asset to my workplace through personal development
- I pride myself on being great at my job
- I will only stop seeking new jobs when I find a career that suits me best
- I find my work to be fun and entertaining
- Getting along with colleagues and customers comes naturally to me
- I accomplish more and more in less time
- Constructive criticism is something I see as helping me grow to my full potential
- Every appointment I go on goes perfectly and I enjoy my time with the client
- I have a 100 percent signing rate
- I am always tentatively on time to work and my appointments.

- I envision my meetings going smoothly and that is why they do
- I am fully mentally and physically prepared for work everyday
- I do more than expected at work and am rewarded for it
- I am honest and dependable in the work place
- I am incredibly punctual in my work
- My customers see me as the expert I am
- I climb the corporate latter with ease
- I am and feel incredibly competent at my craft
- I take pride in my daily actions at work
- I am always the top producer in the work place
- I am extremely knowledgeable about the products and services I offer
- I find joy in the small and mundane tasks along with the big tasks
- I am productive and great at multitasking
- I am so happy I chose this profession
- I reap so many rewards at work, physically and intrinsically
- I ask questions often to help me be the best worker I can
- I am always relaxed and confident at work
- I wholeheartedly believe in whatever I sell
- I voice my opinion at work
- I build long lasting relationships and friendships with my colleagues
- I meet all deadlines with ease
- I feel truly alive at work
- I am never distracted at work
- I close the highest number of sales each month
- I always beat my lasts months numbers
- I am inspired in my work environment
- My work self image gets better and better through all my self development
- I wake up without an alarm because I am excited to go to work

- If I don't believe in something I am selling, I stop immediately and find something I do
- I feel respected at work
- My excitement grows each day at work
- Be Positive
- Speak Up
- Ask For Help
- I am strong
- Listen as much as you speak
- Explain how you feel
- I am a great student
- Be Polite
- I am truthful
- It is safe and OK to express my feelings and goals
- I am creative
- I can do whatever I put my mind to
- I can learn new things
- I enjoy learning about new topics
- I am kind
- I am a hard worker
- I am peaceful
- I seek to understand others
- I am unique
- I am a joyful child of the Lord
- I love making new friends
- I am a leader
- I show others that I care about them
- I am a great listener
- I am forgiving
- I understand my school work and enjoy completing it
- I believe in myself
- I am passionate about life
- I have many abilities
- I am relaxed and calm
- I love life

- I enjoy my own company
- I am perfect as I am
- I am protected
- I am an example student
- I am present in class and in life
- I am the master of my life
- I am loving and compassionate towards friends
- I am a fast and efficient learner
- I see failures as learning and growth experiences
- I am cooperative
- I have a healthy body and mind
- I am a great manager of my time
- I am complete and whole as I am
- I go after my dreams
- Anything is possible
- I have an amazing memory
- I have excellent writing skills
- I am artistic
- I am athletic
- I am always bettering my self
- I love trying new ideas and activities
- I am safe
- I can do it
- My mind is powerful and the key to my dreams
- I have faith in myself
- I love change
- I have a powerful and creative mind
- I reach for the stars
- I help and encourage my family
- I am loved for who I am
- I am an example of love
- I am a great friend to myself
- I am a great friend
- I am persistent
- I have great role models and learn from them

- I expect miracles in my life
- I trust me intuition
- I am handsome/beautiful
- I see the beauty in people
- I see the positive always
- I learn from every experience
- I look forward to each day
- I love challenging myself
- I am limitless
- I am the light of the world
- I have high energy
- I respect my parents and teachers
- I respect myself
- I don't listen to negative people
- I have positive and loving friends
- I create my own destiny
- I have an easy time learning new things
- I am optimistic
- I have wisdom
- I am aloud to be me and express myself
- Everything happens for a reason
- I am adaptive
- I listen to my heart
- I put others before myself
- I see everything in life as exciting and fun
- I enjoy eating healthy
- I am an inspiration to my friends and family
- I am accepting and accept myself every day
- I am limitless talents and gifts that benefit everyone
- I am easy to get along with
- I keep my word no matter what
- I am productive
- I am enough but always striving to be, do and learn more
- I love and accept myself for who I am.
- I radiate and receive love and respect.

- I am loved and respected wherever I go.
- I am unique in my talents and abilities and do not validation from others.
- People see value in my services and I am rewarded graciously.
- I am self-reliant, creative and persistent in whatever I do.
- I deserve all that is good
- I am grateful for all the wonderful things in my life
- I am full of loving, healthy, positive and prosperous thoughts which eventually convert into my life experiences.
- I am unique and my dreams and aspirations are unique to myself. I do not need to prove myself to anyone.
- I am solution driven. Every problem is a chance to grow.
- I am never alone in my pursuit of success. The universe supports me in expected and unexpected ways.
- I am not a prisoner of the past and live only in the moment. That way I enjoy life to the fullest.
- I am not a Tree and have the power to change myself how I see fit.
- Only I am responsible for making my choices and decisions.
- I am not selfish in giving priority to my desires.
- Every moment brings us a choice and I choose happiness no matter what my circumstances.
- I am flexible and open to new experiences.
- I think positively and expect the best.
- I am aware of my strength and act with confidence.
- I can identify my skill gap and act on it.
- Life is beautiful and rewarding.
- Universe blesses me with health, happiness and abundance.
- I appreciate the things I have. I rejoice in the love I receive.
- I am courageous. My eyes reflect the strength of my soul.
- I am positive and optimistic. The universe conspires to make me successful.
- I am passionate about what I do and that reflects by the enthusiasm in my work.

- I attract positive and helping people into my life.
- I am open to meeting people and create positive and supportive relationships.
- I radiate love and inspire people.
- I am calm and peaceful.
- I take time to enjoy the little joys of life.
- I am in full control of my life and in complete harmony with the universe.
- 100 Self Esteem Affirmations That Builds Self Worth
- I am unique. I feel good about being alive and being me.
- Life is fun and rewarding.
- There are no such things as problems, only opportunities.
- I love challenges; they bring out the best in me.
- I replace "I must", "I should" and "I have to" with "I choose". (try it with something you think you have to do, and replace must with choose... notice the difference?)
- I choose to be happy right now. I love my life.
- I appreciate everything I have. I live in joy.
- I am courageous. I am willing to act in spite of any fear.
- I am positive and optimistic. I believe things will always work out for the best.
- It's easy to make friends. I attract positive and kind people into my life.
- It's easy to meet people. I create positive and supportive relationships.
- I am a powerful creator. I create the life I want.
- I am OK as I am. I accept and love myself.
- I am confident. I trust myself.
- I am successful right now.
- I am passionate. I am outrageously enthusiastic and inspire others.
- I have unlimited power at my disposal.
- I am optimistic. I believe things will always work out for the best.

- I am kind and loving. I am compassionate and truly care for others.
- I am focused and persistent. I will never quit.
- I am energetic and enthusiastic. Confidence is my second nature.
- I treat everyone with kindness and respect.
- I inhale confidence and exhale fear.
- I am flexible. I adapt to change quickly.
- I have integrity. I am totally reliable. I do what I say.
- I am competent, smart and able.
- I believe in myself,
- I recognize the many good qualities I have.
- I see the best in other people.
- I surround myself with people who bring out the best in me.
- I let go of negative thoughts and feelings about myself.
- I love who I have become.
- I am always growing and developing.
- My opinions resonate with who I am.
- I am congruent in everything I say and do.
- I deserve to be happy and successful
- I have the power to change myself
- I can forgive and understand others and their motives
- I can make my own choices and decisions
- I am flexible and open to change in every aspect of my life
- I act with confidence having a general plan and accept plans are open to alteration
- It is enough to have done my best
- I deserve to be loved
- I have high self esteem
- I love and respect myself.
- I am a great person.
- I respect myself deeply.
- My thoughts and opinions are valuable.
- I am confident that I can achieve anything.
- I have something special to offer the world.

- Others like and respect me.
- I am a wonderful human being I feel great about myself and my life.
- I am worthy of having high self esteem.
- I believe in myself.
- I deserve to feel good about myself.
- I know I can achieve anything.
- Having respect for myself helps others to like and respect me.
- Feeling good about myself is normal for me.
- Improving my self esteem is very important.
- Being confident in myself comes naturally to me.
- Liking and respecting myself is easy.
- Speaking my mind with confidence is something I just naturally do.
- Each day I notice I am more self discipline.
- I enjoy being self disciplined.
- I am doing the best I can with the knowledge and experience I have obtained so far.
- It's OK to make mistakes. They are opportunities to learn.
- I always follow through on my promises.
- I treat others with kindness and respect.
- I see myself with kind eyes.
- I am fearless.
- I am always improving, but for today, I have the knowledge I need.
- I am calm and mindful.
- I am compassionate with others and myself.
- I am a positive being, aware of my potential.
- There are no blocks I cannot overcome.
- I am strong and wise.
- I love to meet other people and make new friends.
- Life is beautiful.
- I am my best source of motivation.
- Challenges are opportunities to grow and improve.

- I only attract positive people because I am a positive person myself.
- I am unique and that's my Gift to the world.
- I make a difference by showing up every day and doing my best.
- I am becoming a better version of myself one day at a time.
- My actions are intentional and they bring me closer to my goals.
- I deserve what I want because my wish is pure and I have the required qualities.
- I love myself for who I am.
- I totally trust myself.
- I grow in strength with every forward step I take.
- I can do anything I set my mind to do.
- I am capable and strong.
- I am able to easily handle any problem I face.
- When I breathe, I inhale confidence and exhale fear.
- Fear is only a feeling. I can act in the face of fear.
- I release my hesitation and make room for victory.
- I love meeting strangers and I approach them with boldness and enthusiasm.
- I approve of myself and unconditionally deeply love myself.
- I live in the present and am confident of the future.
- My personality exudes confidence. I am bold and outgoing.
- I am self-reliant, creative and persistent in whatever I do.
- I am energetic and enthusiastic. Confidence is my second nature.
- I always attract only the best of circumstances and the best positive people in my life.
- I am a problem solver. I focus on solutions and always find the best solution.
- I love change and easily adjust myself to new situations.
- I love challenges. They bring out the best in me.
- I know that I can master anything. Today I am willing to fail in order to succeed.

- I am proud of myself for even daring to try.
- I am well groomed, healthy and full of confidence. My outer well being is matched by my inner well being.
- Self-confidence is what I thrive on. Nothing is impossible and life is great.
- I feel the love of those who are not physically around me.
- I take pleasure in my own solitude.
- I am too big a gift to this world to feel self-pity.
- I love and approve of myself.
- I focus on breathing and grounding myself.
- Following my intuition and my heart keeps me safe and sound.
- I make the right choices every time.
- I draw from my inner strength and light.
- I am a unique child of this world.
- I have as much brightness to offer the world as the next person.
- I matter and what I have to offer this world also matters.
- I may be one in 7 billion but I am also one in 7 billion.
- I trust my inner wisdom and intuition.
- I breathe in calmness and breathe out nervousness.
- This situation works out for my highest good.
- Wonderful things unfold before me.
- I forgive myself for all the mistakes I have made.
- I let go of my anger so I can see clearly.
- I accept responsibility if my anger has hurt anyone.
- I replace my anger with understanding and compassion.
- I offer an apology to those affected by my anger.
- I may not understand the good in this situation but it is there.
- I muster up more hope and courage from deep inside me.
- I choose to find hopeful and optimistic ways to look at this.
- I kindly ask for help and guidance if I cannot see a better way.
- I refuse to give up because I haven't tried all possible ways.
- I know my wisdom guides me to the right decision.
- I trust myself to make the best decision for me.

- I receive all feedback with kindness but make the final call myself.
- I listen lovingly to this inner conflict and reflect on it until I get to peace around it.
- I love my family even if they do not understand me completely.
- I show my family how much I love them in all the verbal and non-verbal ways I can.
- There is a good reason I was paired with this perfect family.
- I choose to see my family as a gift.
- I am a better person from the hardship that I've gone through with my family.
- I choose friends who approve of me and love me.
- I surround myself with people who treat me well.
- I take the time to show my friends that I care about them.
- My friends do not judge me, nor do they influence what I do with my life.
- I take great pleasure in my friends, even if we disagree or live different lives.
- I am beautiful and smart and that's how everyone sees me.
- I take comfort in the fact that I can always leave this situation.
- I never know what amazing incredible person I will meet next.
- The company of strangers teaches me more about my own likes and dislikes.
- I am doing work that I enjoy and find fulfilling.
- I play a big role in my own career success.
- I ask for and do meaningful, wonderful and rewarding work.
- I engage in work that impacts this world positively.
- I believe in my ability to change the world with the work that I do.
- Peaceful sleep awaits me in dreamland.
- I let go of all the false stories I make up in my head.
- I release my mind of thought until the morning.

- I embrace the peace and quiet of the night.
- I sleep soundly and deeply and beautifully into this night.
- This day brings me nothing but joy.
- Today will be a gorgeous day to remember.
- My thoughts are my reality so I think up a bright new day.
- I fill my day with hope and face it with joy.
- I choose to fully participate in my day.
- I let go of worries that drain my energy.
- I make smart, calculated plans for my future.
- I am a money magnet and attract wealth and abundance.
- I am in complete charge of planning for my future.
- I trust in my own ability to provide well for my family.
- I follow my dreams no matter what.
- I show compassion in helping my loved ones understand my dreams.
- I ask my loved ones to support my dreams.
- I answer questions about my dreams without getting defensive.
- My loved ones love me even without fully grappling with my dreams.
- I accept everyone as they are and continue on with pursuing my dream.
- I am safe and sound. All is well.
- Everything works out for my highest good.
- There is a great reason this is unfolding before me now.
- I have the smarts and the ability to get through this.
- All my problems have a solution.
- I attempt all – not some – possible ways to get unstuck.
- I seek a new way of thinking about this situation.
- The answer is right before me, even if I am not seeing it yet.
- I believe in my ability to unlock the way and set myself free.
- I have no right to compare myself to anyone for I do not know their whole story.
- I compare myself only to my highest self.
- I choose to see the light that I am to this world.

- I am happy in my own skin and in my own circumstances.
- I see myself as a gift to my people and community and nation.
- I am more than good enough and I get better every day.
- I give up the habit to criticize myself.
- I adopt the mindset to praise myself.
- I see the perfection in all my flaws and all my genius.
- I fully approve of who I am, even as I get better.
- I am a good person at all times of day and night.
- I cannot give up until I have tried every conceivable way.
- Giving up is easy and always an option so let's delay it for another day.
- I press on because I believe in my path.
- It is always too early to give up on my goals.
- I must know what awaits me at the end of this rope so I do not give up.
- The past has no power over me anymore
- I embrace the rhythm and the flowing of my own heart.
- All that I need comes to me at the right time and place in this life.
- I am deeply fulfilled with who I am.
- I am becoming more confident in who I am and who I want to be.
- I am a huge gift to this world.
- I forgive myself for any mistakes that I have made.
- I create my own life and have the power to make it amazing.
- My unique talents can benefit others in a great way.
- I have a lot to offer other people.
- My choices are always made perfectly with my best interest at heart.
- I have a wealth of inner-strength to draw from.
- I am never alone in this world and always supported.
- I trust myself to do what is right.
- I am an amazing person.
- I am just as good as everyone else.

- I have an amazing body that helps me do what I need to do each day.
- My body is strong and capable of many things.
- My body is beautiful.
- I always speak to myself in a loving way, just like I would to others.
- I am proud of my body.
- I feel good in my clothes.
- I am perfect with all my imperfections.
- Wanting to be someone else is a waste of the person I am.
- I want to enjoy my life, not focus on my body.
- I refuse to let society tell me how beautiful I am.
- I am a real person, and real is never perfect!
- I don't need to change anything about my body in order to be a beautiful person.
- I am at peace with my life.
- I accept all emotions in my life, but never stay stuck in negative ones.
- I focus on gratitude daily to remind me of how great life is.
- I shine with happiness to everyone I meet.
- I see the humor in all situations and laugh easily.
- I love my home and all that it provides me.
- I enjoy being by myself and cherish my time alone.
- I follow my intuition and always make choices that make me happy.
- I easily let go of my anger because it is useless to me.
- I forgive others so I can stay present where happiness lives.
- I have an overwhelming sense of joy that helps me maintain my happiness.
- I can see the good in everyone and everything.
- I have everything it takes to have the success I want.
- I am living a life that will bring me the success I want.
- Success is my natural birthright.
- I am receiving more and more every day.
- I am following the path that will help me achieve success.

- I easily learn things that help me get to where I want to be.
- I love the job that I am doing.
- I strive to stay aligned with the energy abundance for the highest success possible.
- My actions are always moving me towards more success.
- I am doing great things for the world through my work.
- I allow my intuition to guide me exactly where I need to be.
- I easily attract luck into my life.
- Success flows into my life easily.
- I always turn in my work complete and on time.
- I comprehend what I read quickly.
- I enjoy participating in extracurricular activities.
- I love learning new things and using them in my life.
- I love my classes and my teachers.
- I make excellent grades on quizzes and tests.
- I study comprehensively for my classes.
- I am an excellent employee, always productive and giving my best effort.
- I am experiencing success in my career.
- I enjoy working toward future career success.
- I have a satisfying job.
- I know exactly what I need to do to achieve success in my career.
- My work environment is calm and productive.
- The job I have is perfect for me.
- Every day I become more successful.
- I am successful in my daily life.
- I feel powerful and full of energy, capable and confident.
- I know my success is real.
- I learn from my mistakes and they become stepping stones to my success.
- I love challenges, easily find solutions to problems, and move past roadblocks quickly.
- I am experiencing wealth every day.
- I am financially successful in all my endeavors.

- I am getting wealthier each day.
- I am living the life of my dreams.
- I have enough wealth to fulfil my desires.
- I am confident of my future.
- I am confident, enthusiastic, and energetic.
- My personality shows I am confident.
- I attract confident people.
- I breathe in and out, exhaling hesitancy and inhaling confidence.
- I love change, easily adjusting to new people and situation.
- I love meeting strangers and approach them with boldness and enthusiasm.
- I thrive on self-confidence, knowing that nothing is impossible.
- I am outgoing and make friends easily.
- I am a unique individual, with many special talents and abilities.
- I am attractive, healthy, and confident.
- I am happy with myself the way I am.
- I am proud of myself and the things I have accomplished.
- I am worthy of great things in my life.
- I like myself just the way I am.
- My self-esteem and confidence increases each day.
- All of my thoughts and feelings are under control.
- I awake each day with excitement, awaiting the good things coming to me.
- I breathe in and out, releasing all stress from my body.
- I forgive myself for mistakes and bad decisions I have made.
- I observe my emotions without overreacting.
- I meditate with joy and without resistance or anxiety.
- I reject the idea that I am a prisoner of my emotions and past actions.
- Everything is good right now.
- I accept and embrace all of life's experiences, even the unpleasant ones.

- I am completely in control of my thoughts.
- I am participating in the experiences of the moment.
- I easily return to the present moment and what is happening to me.
- I find joy in the moment.
- I remain engaged and focused on the present moment.
- I know my wisdom and experiences guide me to the right decision.
- I look my options objectively and then make the best decision for me.
- I make the right decision always.
- I receive all advice and feedback with grateful kindness, but I make the final decision myself.
- I trust myself to make the best decisions.
- I am loved beyond comprehension
- I am attracting the perfect mate that my heart desires
- I am grateful for the love that surrounds me
- I emanate love everywhere I go
- I know that to be loved I must love first
- I am so grateful and appreciative for my relationship
- My essence is true love and compassion
- I love my enemies and it makes me feel better
- I am not scared to love
- When I love I live an abundant life
- My heart is open to the possibilities of love
- I have the power to give love constantly
- I have the feeling of love that comes deep from within
- I radiate unconditional love
- I lose nothing and gain everything from giving more love
- I love myself and allow myself to be loved fully
- Love is attracted to me the more I give love
- I love myself
- I lead with love and courage
- My creator loves me
- I attract true love and romance

- I choose love over any other emotion
- I only attract healthy and loving relationships
- I am attracting my soulmate by becoming more loving
- My heart and being is always open to love
- I have an open mindset when it comes to attracting love into my life
- I am loving, loved and lovable.
- There is love all around me
- My relationships are all fulfilling and loving
- I am worthy of loving and being loved
- I have the inner power to offer love endlessly
- Love follows me wherever I go
- I am a love magnet
- I create love and romance in my life with ease
- I seek love and happiness from within so I can manifest it outwards
- I attract and am unconditional love
- I vibrate the vibration of love
- I receive love at all moments of my existence
- Love is powerful and I use it as my greatest tool
- I receive the love back that offer ten times over
- I love my partner and children unconditionally
- Love is my birth right
- I feel the warmth of love fill my heart and soul constantly
- I am completely ready for love to flow in my life
- My soul mate is looking as hard for me as I am looking for them
- I see love in all my visions and memories
- Everyday I wake up I am becoming more loving
- I love myself and people for exactly who they are
- I love my life and love whatever life will bring me
- I naturally find love wherever I go in life
- My relationship lasts a lifetime and are full of love
- I see everything through the eyes of love
- I love like a mother loves their offspring

- I encounter love all day
- I am in a mutually loving relationship
- I don't accept or allow anything unloving to come into my life
- I am so in love with life
- I am always around people who want to love me
- I am in a deeply loving and committed relationship
- I feel the infinite love of the universe in my daily life
- I accept that I am loved
- I don't have to become anything to be loved or attract love, I am perfect as I am
- Love in the most powerful force in the universe
- I receive love and joy in this moment
- Every new friend that I make will bring more love into both of our lives
- My marriage is full of everlasting and infinite love
- I love with every fibber of my being
- My love is like that of a child
- My spouse and family love me for me
- I feel safe and secure since I show love wherever I go
- I move through life with the confidence of knowing that I am loved
- I love romance and it loves and is searching for me
- Romance fills my life with joy and fulfilment
- I spend my energy loving instead of hating
- Unconditional love is where I always operate from
- I deserve to be loved unconditionally
- When I don't feel love outside myself I simply turn inward and love myself
- I feel loved and safe in my partner arms and company
- I express love in all forms
- Everyone is seeking love and I can be that person to bring it to them
- I speak only loving thoughts to my partner
- I love like it is the first time I have ever loved
- I love before I speak

- I love my country
- I love that I have the ability to love and be loved
- I forgive those I condemned with love
- I am open to love on a higher level than I ever expected or wished for
- My soul mate and I will know right away when we meet
- My love life is a priority
- I attract the most loving people into my life
- I focus only on love and beauty
- The right mate is entering my life right now
- I am loving and understanding to my partner
- I will get married or am married to the perfect mate
- My family loves me and supports me no matter what
- There is harmony and loving feelings in my workplace
- People know me as a lover
- I am a manifestation of love
- I am overflowing with love and the feeling of love
- I practice self love on a daily basis
- I overcome fear with ease
- My challenge brings me opportunity that will make me stronger and even more capable
- I release stress because I know it is just energy passing through
- Worry won't change my circumstances; I replace worth with hope
- I am fully capable of overcoming any emotion
- I literally see my stress leaving my body
- I do not resist anxiety, because I know what I resist persists
- I take things one step at a time
- I have beat this before and I will beat this again
- I see my stress and a indicator that I need to look deeper for the cause when it passes
- God listens to my call for help and will get me through
- I am ready to let go
- I envision a still lake when stress arises

- Letting go is not weak it is powerful
- I have the ability to overcome anxiety
- I will not let negative thoughts drain me
- I have everything I need for a happy and stress free life
- I focus on all good in life especially when I feel stressed
- I attract calm situations and people into my life
- I am not my genetics; I don't have to identify with what may run in my family
- I don't identify with this emotion because it's not me
- I don't give anxiety the credit or energy it deserves and it will eventually dissolve
- I am safe here and now
- It feels great to be calm and positive
- I am like water, I move though negative situations with ease by passing through it effortlessly
- I cast all worries to God
- I vibrate at much higher emotion than this anxiety
- I am still
- I am going to be alright
- I am thankful for things in my life when stress arises
- I am relaxed wherever I go
- Each moment my anxiety is slowly disappearing
- I will focus on something else until this passes
- Every time this happens I become stronger and better
- I deflect negative thoughts with ease
- I continue to look forward until I pass through my stress
- I have more control over this than I have every imagined
- I will move away from negativity into the light of positive and optimism
- It is ok to feel this but continue to work on something productive
- I can beat this and see it as a thing of the past
- This is not part of my true identity
- Everyday I am becoming more calm, positive and loving
- I mediate to beat the stress

- I am taken care of by the universe
- I am strong, capable and independent
- I have the power to stop this
- I am not a victim, I am a victor
- I am stronger than I think I am and can show this to myself
- I acknowledge that this is hard but I will persevere
- I love myself and who I am
- I see stress as something not being right and solve this problem in my life with ease
- Stress is pointing me towards my destiny and away from what I do not need in my life
- I love my way through the stressful feelings
- I relax my shoulders and jaw and neck. I see and feel this relaxation flow down through the rest of my body
- I am ok with what is going on in my life right now
- Everything that happens to me will help me grow and help others
- This is not my destiny, I am destined for a peaceful existence
- This is an opportunity to learn and process my thoughts better and more efficient
- Stress wants to beat me but I am the boss of my emotions and they will not win
- I will breathe through this and begin again
- This is teaching me that I can master my own emotions
- Be present, always
- I envision beautiful colors immersed into my stress and anxiety
- I surrender the stress
- I can leave when I feel uncomfortable
- I use exercise as my outlet for stress
- I interpret my emotions; my emotions do not interpret how I react. I can interpret stress as any positive thing I so choose.
- Positive Affirmations For Teens Going Through Those Awkward Years!
- I am wise, I learn from all situations and scenarios

- This too shall pass
- I am perfectly complete and show compassion to myself daily
- I see failure as feedback, not something to hold me back
- My path is guided and I will trust the process
- I love the feeling of growth in my daily life
- Nobody is perfect and I embrace my flaws
- I am encouraging because it makes me feel stronger
- I am above all of the drama
- Everyday is the best day of my life
- I am passionate about life
- I am young and enjoy my youthfulness
- I embrace the awkward times by laughing them off
- I am hopefully
- I have great study habits
- I am always having a wonderful day
- I only get more successful from every setback
- I am a born winner
- I am a great athlete and develop my abilities daily through hard work and self belief
- I follow my dreams with relentless pursuit regardless of what people say
- I am a visionary of the perfect future I am creating
- I see great qualities in everyone
- My teachers see the value in me and know I am unique
- I seek to understand people before offering my opinion
- I enjoy being the top of my class
- I look my best daily because it creates great self confidence
- You are incredibly capable
- I am an awesome test taker
- I feel relaxed and at ease on test days
- I maintain full attention in class
- I am special
- I am not phased by other people's opinions about me
- I create my circumstances and only manifest what I desire
- I seek to learn and grow into the person I want to become

- I can improve daily and do so with ease
- I overcome challenges with ease
- My friends see me as a leader and someone they can confide
- Everything happens for a reason
- I help others and enjoy doing so
- I am peaceful and positive
- My mind is unlimited and always concentrated on my task at hand
- I have an open mind to all the possibilities in my life
- I see beauty where others don't
- I only compete with myself and will beat my old self daily
- My habits create self discipline that inspires confidence in me
- All is well, everything is happening exactly the way it should
- What people fret over, I laugh at
- I have an abundant amount of talents and gifts
- I deal with my fears calmly and effectively
- I find learning exciting and enjoyable
- I am a fast learner
- I enjoy partaking in my passions
- I am free to think how I choose
- I am well organized
- I see my creativity as the perfect outlet I can use you relax
- I am a problem solver
- My strong intuition guides me daily
- I love the passionate and creative people that surround me
- I deserve love, success and kindness to flow through my life
- I feel empowered daily because I know I am becoming better and better
- I see myself as a maverick and a person of value
- I create healthy and beneficial relationships with my teachers
- I enjoy working with my fellow students in pursuit of knowledge and growth
- I do not have attachments on outcomes because everything is happening for a purpose
- My goals are reached easily

- I am on a journey and see life as fun and interesting
- I release the past and live in the present on a daily basis
- I honor and trust myself with every decision I make
- I am worthy of the love and respect I receive from others
- Although I may feel lost, it is in indicator that I use to find the best way in life
- I offer my care and affection with my whole heart
- I love the feeling of youth and will retain it for all my days
- I focus on solutions in my life
- My nature is courage and confidence
- I as well as others believe in me and my abilities
- I seek knowledge on my own terms because I know it is power
- I am wonderful
- I am brilliant, clever and funny
- I utilize my gifts to bring myself and others happiness
- I am sexy and good looking and I own it
- I feel included, needed and respected
- I accept about me what others don't
- I am prosperous and abundant
- I do not resist change and let go of what doesn't serve me
- I live in a state of fulfilment
- I know that happiness is my true nature so I enjoy myself at all times
- I am free to take the path of my heart
- I listen to my heart
- I am here for a purpose
- My life is a series of events leading to my destiny
- I love feeling out of place sometimes because I know that is where growth takes place
- I keep my composure when I receive opposition
- I am a person of my word
- I have a plan for my life
- I expect great things to happen to me in unexpected ways
- I am a gift to my friends, family and self

- I make this world a better place
- I know my flaws are beautiful and make me special
- I only see the good in others and myself
- I adjust effortlessly to change
- I love and accept in the here and now
- I believe in my abilities and skills
- My mistakes are seen as growing and learning opportunities
- I wholeheartedly believe in myself
- I am a beautiful creation
- I am positive and courageous. I act in spite of fear
- I accept and deeply love who I am
- I am passionate and I am an inspiration to others
- I persevere though anything in my life
- I will never ever quit
- I treat myself and others with kindness and compassion
- I am successful here and now and will only get more successful
- I am constantly seeking growth to better myself
- I know that happiness comes within and that is where I seek happiness and love
- I see the best in myself and in people
- I exhale all thoughts and negative and destructive feelings and inhale positivity and courageousness
- I have the power to transform myself and shred my old skin
- I am a person of my word and people respect me for it
- I see all the good qualities in myself and the bad ones I only see them as how I can better myself though
- I have power over my emotions, they do not control me
- I am a fearless leader
- I embrace change and love who I am becoming through it
- I deserve all the good things live has to offer
- I am self disciplined and it shows up everywhere in my life
- I enjoy high self confidence and do not see it as arrogance
- I deserve to feel powerful and confident
- I respect my body and my mind and treat it accordingly

- I only choose to love myself more and more daily
- I am respected my peers
- I am unique and love that fact about me
- I attract loving relationships because I am being myself and people love that about me
- I am capable of anything. Capable of miracles
- I attract self confident friends in my life that only better me
- I am a great person
- I am a powerhouse of productivity
- I believe in myself so deeply
- My faith in myself is unshakable
- I achieve everything that my soul is aligned with
- I am so much to offer to this world and will do so
- I am constantly aligning myself with my life purpose
- I combat negative thoughts with empowering thoughts
- Confidence comes natural to me
- I learn and grow daily
- I am my own best friend; I am here for me. I have my own back.
- I know that to be more I must become more through growth
- I love reshaping my body because it makes me feel great about myself
- I eat healthy because I show power over my self and it gives me vitality and high energy
- I love the individual I am becoming
- My life means something and I see that meaning everywhere I go
- I have great ideas and collaborate with like minded people to make those ideas a reality
- I am worthy
- I am unique
- I am constantly improving myself and love what it does to my self confidence
- I let go of all limiting beliefs

- I see peoples opinions as just that, opinions that don't have to become my reality
- I have access to anything I need to succeed and feel confident in myself
- I see life as a classroom where I am constantly learning and developing myself
- I have the power to change myself
- I deserve to be loved
- I have done my best and that is enough
- I form my own options and decisions
- I am deserving of all that is good and abundant
- I love myself because I know happiness comes from within
- I accept myself fully and unconditionally
- I feel so good about my life
- I am beautiful
- Every time I catch myself thinking low of myself I vow to replace that thought with a positive one
- I create happiness in my life daily
- I attract scenarios that allow me to feel empowered
- I ooze self confidence
- I attract people help me on my journey to untouchable self confidence
- I love feeling my high self esteem
- My self esteem is a reflection of my growth, I know this and will grow beyond measure
- I better myself daily because I love myself and want to create the best me
- I am always making positive changes in my life
- My potentially is limitless
- I free myself from the people that have hurt me
- I forgive myself and always show myself compassion
- I feel so vibrant and healthy living this life
- I feel grateful for being myself
- I embrace my good and bad qualities

- I integrate things into my day that reinforce habits that create excellent self esteem
- I'm still a good person even though I may have done bad things
- My life has purpose
- Compassion washes over me when I am angry
- I always stand up for myself. I would rather stand alone then in a crowd of sheep
- Positive habits are all that consume my day
- Happiness is a choice and I choose it every day
- My thoughts always default to the positive
- I can't change anything or anyone outside myself
- I have divine destiny that is unfolding every day
- This too shall pass
- I feel peace at all times and feel at peace with the world
- I take what people say about me with a grain of salt
- I am proud of the person I am becoming
- I give myself permission to be myself and act like myself with caring what others think
- I mediate on high self esteem when I feel lack of self worth
- The vision of me feeling high self esteem is my anchor I go to often to transform my self image
- I have the power to manifest anything I want in this life with the power of my mind
- I am so grounded in the belief in myself that nothing and no one can touch me!
- I always see only the good in others.
- I attract only positive people.
- I face difficult situations with courage and conviction.
- I always find a way out of such situations.
- I love and accept myself unconditionally.
- I am a deserving human being.
- I approve of myself and feel great about myself.
- I radiate love and respect and in return I get love and respect.
- I am well loved and well respected.

- My high self-esteem enables me to respect others and get respect back in return.
- I have the strength to make my dreams come true.
- I am free to make my own choices and decisions.
- I am a unique and a very special person and worthy of respect from others.
- I like myself better and better each and every day.
- My high self-esteem allows me to accept compliments easily and also freely compliment others.
- I accept others as they are and they in turn accept me as I am.
- It matters little what others say. What matters is how I react and what I believe.
- All is well in my world and I trade love and acceptance with the world.
- I consciously release the past and live only in the present. That way I get to enjoy and experience life to the full.
- I have high self-esteem as I respect myself.
- I am a winner! I deserve all that is good.
- I release any need for misery and suffering.
- I release the need to prove myself to anyone as I am my own self and I love it that way.
- I am solution minded. Any problem that comes up in life is solvable.
- I am never alone. The universe supports me and is with me at every step.
- My mind is filled only with loving, healthy, positive and prosperous thoughts, which ultimately are converted into my life experiences.
- My mind is full of gratitude for my lovely and wonderful life.
- I am solution-driven. I am not afraid of obstacles.
- I am capable of accomplishing my tasks and responsibilities.
- I am grateful for my journey and its lessons.
- I have unlimited power.
- I love myself and the circumstances life presents me.
- I accept compliments easily because I know I deserve them.

- Everything is possible.
- I am creative and open to new solutions.
- I am talented and intelligent.
- My work fulfils me.
- I acknowledge my Super Powers and use them to assist others.
- I am enthusiastic, confident and persistent.
- I let go of fearing mistakes and failure
- The more I like myself, the more others will like me.
- I am becoming better with each day.
- I am happy to be here.
- I have people who care about me and will help me if I need it.
- I will ask for help if I need it.
- I am always learning more about who I am and what matters to me.
- I understand that my actions become habits so I will try to do the right thing.
- I love and respect my family for all they do for me.
- I am an intelligent being, but I don't know everything.
- I am proud to represent the values that matter to me and my community.
- I love myself.
- I feel lucky to have the opportunities that I do.
- My dreams are achievable.
- The only people who may be judging me, are the people who are most afraid of being judged.
- In 5 years it is not going to matter what I wore today.
- In 15 years the only thing that will remain is what I have learned.
- My first love will probably not be my only love, and I'm ok with that.
- People can be mean, but it only reflects the kind of person they are.
- I am happy. Who else am I trying to please?

- I accept and love the way I look without comparing myself to others.
- A six-pack does not need to be standard. In either form.
- I am completely unique and therefore, there are no rules to what I am and am not.
- I give myself permission to do what is best for me.
- I admit that I may not always know what is best for me, so I am open to advice from people who I respect.
- I do not need drugs or alcohol to have fun.
- I do not need to share every personal detail with my entire social network.
- I am responsible with my technology.
- My opinion matters.
- I acknowledge that sometimes it is not appropriate to voice my opinion.
- I care about what is going on in the world.
- I can say no, and no will mean no.
- I stand up for myself because I matter.
- I love myself unconditionally.
- I see the beauty in stopping to appreciate my blessings.
- I am not in a race, there is plenty of time.
- Reputation is important, but it is not defining.
- My friends are not always right.
- I am not lost, I'm still creating myself.
- When there is a bump in the road, I keep going.
- If someone is trying to bring me down, it means I am above them.
- I have all the tools to be successful.
- Though times may be difficult, they will eventually get better.
- I do not regret yesterday and I am excited for tomorrow.
- This is only the beginning.
- I will do better next time.
- I haven't even seen what I am capable of yet.
- I will savor my youth.
- I do not wish for age but instead experiences and knowledge.

- I will do today what I will appreciate tomorrow.
- I am the architect of my life. I am the creator of my reality.
- I accept and love myself just the way I am.
- I am supported and loved by God (or: the Creator/Universe/etc.)
- I am surrounded by abundance.
- I am healthy, energetic and optimistic.
- I am overflowing with happiness, joy and satisfaction.
- My body is relaxed. My mind is calm. My soul is at peace.
- I am able to achieve whatever I desire.
- I transcendent negativity.
- I can achieve greatness.
- Everything happens for a reason. Everything leads to something positive.
- I am forgiving. My compassion replaces anger with love.
- I am able to conquer all the challenges I am confronted with.
- I am becoming more confident and stronger each day.
- My potential to succeed is infinite.
- I am becoming more knowledgeable and wiser with each day.
- I am creative and bursting with brilliant ideas.
- I am courageous and overcome my fears by confronting them.
- I am at peace with my past.
- I radiate love, happiness, grace and positivity
- I am patient, diplomatic and tolerant.
- I am grateful for the wonders in my life.
- The universe supports me in every possible way.
- Every experience in my life helps me to grow.
- Today I lay the foundation for a wonderful future.
- I am safe and protected by divinity.
- I speak kindly of others.
- Everything I seek can be found within.
- I set myself free by forgiving myself.
- I am significant. I contribute to the advancement of humankind.

- Affirmations for Self-Esteem
- I love myself and feel great about myself.
- I accept myself unconditionally.
- I see problems as interesting challenges.
- I radiate confidence.
- Challenges bring out the best in me.
- I have confidence in my abilities and skills.
- I make sound decisions.
- I am bold and courageous.
- I face difficulty with courage.
- I am worthy of happiness and love.
- I am confident, happy, healthy, and powerful.
- I believe in myself and my capabilities.
- I deserve everything I want in life.
- I love myself unconditionally.
- Every day I am becoming a better version of myself.
- I deserve love.
- I deserve happiness.
- I deserve success.
- Life is beautiful.
- Today is a great day to be alive!
- Success and abundance are my birth right.
- I am attracting positive people and circumstances into my life.
- I am a strong and powerful person.
- I am naturally confident and at ease in my own life.
- Being confident comes naturally to me.
- I am worthy, wonderful, and wise.
- I am compassionate, kind, and courageous.
- My gifts are one-of-a-kind and unique to me.
- I feel confident when I speak up for myself.
- My authentic self is of immense value to the world.
- I have unique and valuable gifts to offer the world.
- I am confident, happy, healthy, and in alignment with my life.
- I am clear and confident in my personal choices.

- I believe in my capabilities.
- I am worthy, wise, and wonderful. Confidence comes naturally to me.
- Confidence comes naturally to me when I share my gifts and talents with the world.
- My body, mind, and spirit are powerful and profound.
- I am outgoing and confident. I share my love with the world.
- I am relaxed, kind, peaceful, and confident.
- Every day my confidence is growing.
- I am succeeding in life.
- I have a great deal of respect for myself.
- I only attract other people who respect and appreciate me.
- I am attracting abundance and joy into my life.
- I know I can achieve anything I want in life.
- I am motivated, positive, and confident in my life vision.
- I have complete confidence in myself and my path.
- I am confident, courageous, and compassionate.
- I go confidently in the direction of my dreams.
- I am calm, clear, courageous, and confident.
- I am courageous, content, and confident.
- I am confident in my athletic abilities and skills.
- I am confident in my skills and gifts.
- I am confident that my gifts and talents are of great benefit to the world.
- I have full confidence in myself and my abilities.
- I radiate love and self confidence.
- I face challenging situations with confidence, courage, and conviction.
- I live in the present wonderful moment and trust in my future.
- I am confident in my unique gifts and talents and I share them proudly with the world.
- I am humble yet confident.
- I feel good.
- I am happy to be alive.

- I begin my day by affirming the positive and end my day with gratitude.
- I have strong self esteem and I love to socialize and celebrate life.
- My attitude is so brimming with self esteem that I attract like minded people.
- Every day in every way I am growing more confident and filled with self esteem.
- When I breathe deeply my confidence and self esteem expand.
- I am now fearless, courageous, bold, and filled with awesome self esteem.
- My unique talents flow through me and supercharge my self esteem.
- I am a focused and action orientated individual with loads of self esteem.
- I have a magnetic and dynamic personality overflowing with self esteem.
- I now walk with assurance, poise, strength, and a full tank of self esteem.
- My contacts with people are smooth because I now utilize my self esteem.
- My character appeals to everyone because they sense my strong self esteem.
- My expression communicates certainty, confidence, and loads of self esteem.
- I am friendly, outgoing, confident, and exploding with positive self esteem.
- I now make good friends quickly and easily using my heightened self esteem.
- I am excited around others because they can sense my heightened self esteem.
- Other people believe in me because my self esteem is so strong can't be ignored.
- I am now positively adventurous and filled with outrageous self esteem.

- I am more attractive and confident every day because of my strong self esteem.
- I increase my self esteem by increasingly putting my skills into action every day.
- My self esteem is so strong I provide support and confidence others in need.
- I get the benefit of the doubt because people notice my growing self esteem.
- I easily connect with everyone I meet because of my expanding self esteem.
- Regardless of their status I look others in the eye with full self esteem.
- I now radiate self esteem and certainty in the presence of other people.
- I use my self esteem to control the pictures, sounds, and thoughts in my mind.
- All my facial expressions are based in self esteem and are pleasant to others.
- Everyone appreciates who I am and the high self esteem I have achieved.
- Other people feel my enhanced self esteem and think I'm an interesting person.
- My confidence, competence, and self esteem are exploding massively every day.
- I move my body with confidence while displaying awesome self esteem.
- Good people are attracted to me every day now that I have magnetic self esteem.
- The advantage is always mine now that I'm completely filled with self esteem.
- People want to be like me because my confidence and self esteem are contagious.
- I mentally rehearse the results I want so my skill and self esteem expand wildly.
- My sense of humor and self esteem touches everyone around me.

- I am a strong and charismatic personality filled to the rim with self esteem.
- I have more than enough strength, vigor, and self esteem to complete my goals.
- People subconsciously notice my heightened self esteem and are attracted to it.
- My great ideas, energy, and self esteem create opportunities out of nowhere.
- I embrace success. The words "I can't" are not in my vocabulary. I refuse to believe my own excuses. I am unstoppable!
- I am calm in the face of conflict. I brush annoyances off quickly & easily. I agree to disagree. I am bigger than that!
- I choose to radiate love, joy & gratitude today. I know life is too short to dwell on negativity. I walk in the light!
- I release my need to impress others. I know that I have nothing to prove. I choose to accept myself just the way I am!
- I am free to create my OWN reality. I have choices in all situations. Nothing stands between me and my highest good.
- I release my attachment to everything that no longer serves me. I refuse to let anything or anyone hold me back!
- I release my need to compare myself to others. I judge myself by my own standards of success. I am ENOUGH just as I am.
- I am ready to show the world who I am and what I have to offer. No one can stop me from fulfilling my purpose!
- I am making space for more success to come into my life. I let go of my excuses. I am productive & focused on results!
- I choose to take responsibility for my own happiness. I will not let anyone "make" me angry today. I am in control!
- I am committed to the possibility of my own success. I take action on my goals now so I can have the lifestyle I want.
- I honor my need to rest and recharge. I am committed to finding at least one hour of "me" time today!
- I am here for a reason. That reason does not include gossip & negativity. I am committed to being a positive influence!

- I take my goals seriously. I know that my time here on earth is limited. I honor my life by doing what I love.
- I am committed to my own success. I go out of my way to meet people I admire & respect. I am on the path to greatness!
- I am comfortable asking for what I want because I know I deserve it. I choose to honor my desires today and always.
- I release all negativity from my life. I choose to focus on being positive and productive!
- I am thankful for this beautiful day and the infinite possibility it holds. I know something good is going to happen!
- I allow myself to be open to new opportunities and possibilities. I am free of believing that my options are limited.
- I can achieve whatever I want. I can have what I desire. Everything is possible.
- No matter what happens today, I will remember the truth that I am beautiful, powerful and free.
- I trust my inner wisdom and intuition. I am the only one who knows what's best for me.
- I am focused on doing what I was put here on earth to do. Everything else is a distraction.
- I release my attachment to everything that no longer serves me. I deserve to be happy and free.
- Instead of complaining about not having ENOUGH time today, I will use the time I DO have in a way that honors my values and goals.
- As soon as I commit to my ideal life, the universe will start moving on my behalf. All I have to do is take the first step.
- My life is free from drama and negativity. I surround myself with love and light.
- I am brave enough to embrace my true power. I have full control over my life.
- Regardless of the situations which confront me, I know that I am blessed. I receive the blessing from every lesson!

- I release my desire to be "perfect." I am already good enough to be loved & accepted. I know I am worthy just as I am!
- Forgiveness is a gift I give myself. By forgiving others, I set myself free from pain & suffering. I choose to forgive.
- Even if I take a wrong turn, I can find another route. I can get a map & chart a new course. Stopping is not an option!
- I am committed to accomplishing my goals, despite all the mistakes I make along the way. I choose to LEARN from them!
- I release all feelings of envy. I am destined to live my OWN version of happy that has nothing to do with anyone else.
- I will plant only GOOD seeds in the world today. I will not waste even one precious second in anger, hate or jealousy.
- I embrace my BEST self today. I choose to live in a way that will bring peace, joy, and happiness to myself and others.
- I am right where I need to be. I embrace the challenges & opportunities facing me right now. I choose to learn & grow!
- I am the President of my life. I refuse to allow anyone else to play that role. I trust myself to make good decisions.
- I release my need to control the future. Instead, I simply focus on allowing the BEST to happen!
- I choose to let go of the OLD so that I can finally start making progress with the NEW path I want to take in my life.
- I honor my desire to reach my goals. By doing at least ONE thing everyday, I make consistent progress toward my dreams!
- Instead of being discouraged by how far I still have left to go, I choose to be grateful for how far I've already come.
- I know that I was put on earth for a purpose. I choose to honor that purpose today & inspire others to walk their path.
- I refuse to allow myself to be overcommitted. I say NO quickly and easily. I protect my "me time" because I deserve it.
- I release all feelings of jealousy. I know I am enough & have enough. I don't have to compete with anyone for anything.

- I embrace the infinite possibility of today. I am enthusiastic about life & ready to take inspired action on my goals!
- I refuse to allow others to hold me back from doing what I really want to do. I give myself permission to walk MY path.
- I accept the truth that the past cannot be changed. I choose to focus on my future and move forward in the light.
- I embrace my full potential, even if it makes others uncomfortable. I refuse to play small. I'm meant to do BIG things.
- I am no longer afraid of the unknown because I know I can overcome ANY challenge that comes my way. I am invincible!
- I choose to be myself & allow others to be themselves. I know I am no better than anyone else. We are ALL on the path.
- I release all negative thoughts. I maintain a positive mindset despite challenges. I give myself permission to SHINE!
- I embrace this opportunity to be better than I was yesterday. I take responsibility for my choices today and always.
- I choose to take action in spite of my fear of failure. No matter what happens, I give myself credit for daring to try.
- I am committed to taking action in spite of fear, knowing that all of my needs will be taken care of by the universe.
- I have nothing to worry about. I choose to focus only on what I can control. The rest will work itself out for my good.
- I don't need the approval of others because I approve of myself. I know that my approval is the only kind that matters.
- I am in the right place at the right time. I am on the right path and I trust myself to make the right decisions.
- Instead of judging others, I judge myself on whether I'm being the best I can be. It's always a better use of my time.
- I am in control of my life. I don't need anyone's approval before I make a decision. I choose to do what's best for ME.
- I am in charge of my own happiness. I let go of the belief that I need someone to "make" me happy.
- I don't have to wait until I feel "ready" to take action on my goals. The timing will never be perfect. I am ready now.

- No one can make me angry. I am responsible for my emotions and reactions. I choose to be at peace.
- There is nothing wrong with me. I am not lacking in any way. I am good enough. I have enough. I AM enough.
- I know what I want. I know I deserve to have it. I take responsibility for bringing it into my life.
- I am beautiful and worthy of every truly beautiful thing.
- I am ready to let go of everything that no longer serves me. I choose to walk the bright path to my own happiness.
- Fear flows through me but it is not me. I am bigger than fear. I am beyond fear. Fear does not define me. I am not fear.
- I am willing to forgive. Forgiving myself and others releases me from the pain of the past. I forgive and I am free.
- I accept responsibility for my own happiness. I don't need anyone or anything to complete me because I am already complete.

The list of affirmation is now over; we are now going to continue with new affirmations to elevate your feeling of Self-Empowerment with a quick explanation for each that will help you to understand the under layer meaning.

Affirmations for Self-Empowerment

- "I am worthy."

Simple but powerful. This affirmation reminds you that you have every right to ask to receive everything you want, no matter what undermining messages you may have received in earlier life.

- "I have all the power I need."

Sometimes, we think we need to rely on others in order to get what we want. While other people can be great resources and supporters, it's important to understand that you have everything you need inside.

- "I make my dreams my reality."

A statement like this is a good way to quickly reflect on the truth of the Law of Attraction. And to turn your attention to your endless ability to shape the world around you.

- "I give my unique gifts to the world."

Instead of comparing yourself to other people and worrying that you come up short, see that no one can give the world what you do. Rejoice in the fact that you are enriching that world every day.

- "I contain multitudes."

You will sometimes have mixed feelings, and you will change and evolve over time. Both of these things are okay! They simply reflect your complexity. Respect and honor your many facets, and all they have to teach you.

- "I will be my own best advocate."

Just as you already have all the power you need, you should feel confident about advocating for your needs and goals. You don't need to apologize to anyone for pursuing respect and success. This affirmation helps you stay in tune with that idea.

- "I have the strength to succeed."

These words are useful whether you need to empower yourself to work towards abundance, romance, a rich career or something else entirely. This is a quick affirmation to use when you're feeling a little wobbly.

- "I am the author of my own destiny."

No one else gets to decide what's best for you, what you want, or how you pursue it. Say this sentence to combat the underlying worry that you need to please others or that you should bow to their expertise in matters of your own happiness.

- "I am responsible for my own happiness."

Likewise, no one gets to take away your joy. Plus, no one can be blamed for preventing you from having it. Happiness is a choice, and it's one you can make today.

- "I give and receive love each day."

Compassion and love boost your vibrational frequency and attract better things into your life, so a morning affirmation like this sets you up for a day of reciprocal positivity.

- "I will triumph over all challenges."

There is nothing you can't overcome! However, sometimes you need to hear yourself say this out loud before you remember that it really is true.

- "I have the power to choose."

Sometimes, it can feel like you're being forced into a corner, by people or by circumstance. However, your own manifestation abilities mean that you can always choose to do something different. Plus, realizing this is freeing.

- "To take care of others, I need to take care of myself."

Whenever you feel like you're draining your own resources to meet the needs of others, this affirmation can push you to see that you need to put your self-care first

- "I believe in myself."

Finally, sometimes the simplest affirmations are the very best. If you verbalize your trust and belief in yourself often enough, it will become the bedrock upon which all your other decisions are made.

The Self-Empowerment affirmation are now over. I hope you enjoyed this format.

Next, we are going to listen to Quotes about Self-Esteem.

QUOTES FOR SELF-ESTEEM

Get yourself ready as I will be starting the best quotes to boost your self-esteem and motivate you in your day to day life:

- "You yourself, as much as anybody in the entire universe, deserve your love and affection." ~ Buddha
- "Your chances of success in any undertaking can always be measured by your belief in yourself." ~ Robert Collier
- "The strongest single factor in prosperity consciousness is self-esteem: believing you can do it, believing you deserve it, believing you will get it." ~ Jerry Gillies
- "There is overwhelming evidence that the higher the level of self-esteem, the more likely one will be to treat others with respect, kindness, and generosity." ~ Nathaniel Branden
- "The golden opportunity you are seeking is in yourself. It is not in your environment, it is not in luck or chance, or the help of others; it is in yourself alone." ~ Orison Swett Marden
- "Listen to your heart above all other voices." ~ Marta Kagan
- "Always be a first-rate version of yourself, instead of a second-rate version of somebody else." ~ Judy Garland
- "You were not born a winner, and you were not born a loser. You are what you make yourself be." ~ Lou Holtz
- "Self-trust is the first secret of success." ~ Ralph Waldo Emerson
- "The most important opinion you have is the one you have of yourself, and the most significant things you say all day are those things you say to yourself."
- "No one can make you feel inferior without your consent." ~ Eleanor Roosevelt
- "Trust yourself. Create the kind of self that you will be happy to live with all your life. Make the most of yourself by fanning the tiny, inner sparks of possibility into flames of achievement." ~ Golda Meir

- "Someone else's opinion of you does not have to become your reality." ~ Les Brown
- "I was always looking outside myself for strength and confidence but it comes from within. It is there all the time." ~ Anna Freud
- "If I am not for myself, who will be?" ~ Pirke Avoth
- "The tragedy is that so many people look for self-confidence and self-respect everywhere except within themselves, and so they fail in their search." ~ Dr. Nathaniel Branden
- "It took me a long time not to judge myself through someone else's eyes." ~ Sally Field
- "The way you treat yourself sets the standard for others." ~ Dr. Sonya Friedman
- "There is only one corner of the universe you can be certain of improving, and that's your own self." ~ Aldous Leonard Huxley
- "You have within you right now, everything you need to deal with whatever the world can throw at you." ~ Brian Tracy
- "Aerodynamically the bumblebee shouldn't be able to fly, but the bumblebee doesn't know that so it goes on flying anyway." ~ Mary Kay Ash
- "If you doubt you can accomplish something, then you can't accomplish it. You have to have confidence in your ability, and then be tough enough to follow through." ~ Rosalyn Smith Carter
- "Confidence comes not from always being right but from not fearing to be wrong." ~ Peter Mcintyre
- "We have to learn to be our own best friends because we fall too easily into the trap of being our own worst enemies." ~ Roderick Thorp
- "It ain't what they call you, it's what you answer to." ~ W.C. Fields
- "Whether you think you can or think you can't – you are right." ~ Henry Ford

- "I am convinced all of humanity is born with more gifts than we know. Most are born geniuses and just get de-geniused rapidly." ~ Buckminster Fuller
- "If you really put a small value upon yourself, rest assured that the world will not raise your price."
- "Thousands of geniuses live and die undiscovered – either by themselves or by others." ~ Mark Twain
- "Nothing splendid has ever been achieved except by those who dared believe that something inside of them was superior to circumstance." ~ Bruce Barton
- "Always act like you're wearing an invisible crown."
- "What a man thinks of himself, that it is which determines, or rather indicates his fate." ~Henry David Thoreau
- "The best way to gain self-confidence is to do what you are afraid to do."
- "Our deepest fear is not that we are inadequate. Our deepest fear is that we are powerful beyond measure. It is our light, not our darkness that most frightens us. We ask ourselves, Who am I to be brilliant, gorgeous, talented, fabulous? Actually, who are you not to be? You are a child of God. Your playing small does not serve the world. There is nothing enlightened about shrinking so that other people won't feel insecure around you. We are all meant to shine, as children do. We were born to make manifest the glory of God that is within us. It is not just in some of us; it is in everyone. And as we let our own light shine, we unconsciously give other people permission to do the same. As we are liberated from our own fear, our presence automatically liberates others." ~ Marianne Williamson
- "Well, we all know that self-esteem comes from what you think of you, not what other people think of you." ~ Gloria Gaynor
- "To trust one's mind and to know that one is worthy of happiness is the essence of self-esteem." ~ Nathaniel Branden

- "Too many people overvalue what they are not, and undervalue what they are." ~ Malcolm Forbes
- "Of all the judgments we pass in life, none is more important than the judgment we pass on ourselves". ~ Nathaniel Branden.
- "One of the most significant characteristics of healthy esteem is that it is the state of one who is not at war either with himself or with others". ~ Nathaniel Branden.
- "The most important key to the permanent enhancement of esteem is the practice of positive inner-talk". ~ Dennis Waitley.
- "The greatest success is successful self-acceptance." ~ Ben Sweet
- "Love is the great miracle cure. Loving ourselves works miracles in our lives." ~ Louise L. Hay.
- "To have an incredible increase in self esteem, all you have to do is start doing some little something. You don't have to do spectacularly dramatic things for self esteem to start going off the scale. Just make a commitment to any easy discipline. Then another one and another one." ~ Jim Rohn
- "Self worth cannot be verified by others. You are worthy because you say it is so. If you depend on others for your value it is other-worth." ~ Wayne Dyer
- "Persons of high self esteem are not driven to make themselves superior to others; they do not seek to prove their value by measuring themselves against a comparative standard. Their joy is being who they are, not in being better than someone else." ~ Nathaniel Branden
- "Having a low opinion of yourself is not 'modesty'. It's self-destruction. Holding your uniqueness in high regard is not 'egotism'. It's a necessary precondition to happiness and success." ~ Bobbe Sommer
- "Tell me how a person judges his or her self esteem and I will tell you how that person operates at work, in love, in sex, in parenting, in every important aspect of existence – and how high he or she is likely to rise. The reputation you have with

yourself – your self-esteem – is the single most important factor for a fulfilling life." ~ Nathaniel Branden
- "Never bend your head. Hold it high. Look the world straight in the eye." ~ Helen Keller
- "Today you are you, that is truer than true. There is no one alive who is youer than you." ~ Dr. Seuss
- "People are like stained-glass windows. They sparkle and shine when the sun is out, but when the darkness sets in their true beauty is revealed only if there is light from within." ~ Elisabeth Kübler-Ross

The first place where self-esteem begins its journey is within us. — Stephen Richards

- Confidence comes from discipline and training. – Robert Kiyosaki
- Your mind is a powerful thing. When you fill it with positive thoughts, your life will start to change.
- Confidence is something you create in yourself by believing in who you are.
- Don't let your fear of what could happen make nothing happen.
- The pain you feel today will be the strength you feel tomorrow.
- Choices
- Attitude is a choice.
- Happiness is a choice.
- Optimism is a choice.
- Kindness is a choice.
- Giving is a choice.
- Respect is a choice.
- Whatever choice you make makes you.
- Choose wisely.
- — Roy T. Bennett
- Love yourself first and everything else falls into line. You really have to love yourself to get anything done in this world. – Lucille Ball

- Identify your problems, but give your power and energy to solutions. – Tony Robbins
- No matter who you are, no matter what you did, no matter where you've come from, you can always change, and become a better version of yourself. – Madonna
- You don't have to be arrogant to be confident. Some of the most humblest people in the world are confident. So stand tall. Speak up. And live the life of your dreams. You deserve it just as equally as everyone else does. – Unknown
- Character cannot be developed in ease and quiet. Only through experience of trial and suffering can the soul be strengthened, ambition inspired, and success achieved. – Helen Keller
- Learn from the past, set vivid, detailed goals for the future, and live in the only moment of time over which you have any control: now. – Denis Waitley
- In essence, if we want to direct our lives, we must take control of our consistent actions. It's not what we do once in a while that shapes our lives, but what we do consistently. – Tony Robbins
- A strong person is not the one who doesn't cry. A strong person is the one who cries and shed tears for a moment, then gets up and fights again.
- Happiness is a choice, not a result. Nothing will make you happy until you choose to be happy. No person will make you happy unless you decide to be happy. Your happiness will not come to you. It can only come from you. – Ralph Harslon
- Love who you are, embrace who you are. Love yourself. When you love yourself, people can kind of pick up on that: they can see confidence, they can see self-esteem, and naturally, people gravitate towards you. – Lilly Singh
- The greatest "mistake" you can make in life is to be continually fearing you will make one. – E Hubbard
- Somebody should tell us...right at the start of our lives...that we are dying. Then we might live to the limit,

every minute of every day. Do it! I say. Whatever you want to do, do it now! There are only so many tomorrows.
– Michael Landon

- You ready?
- Never quit.
- If you stumble get back up.
- What happened yesterday no longer matters.
- Today's another day.
- So get back on track and
- Move closer to your dreams and goals.
- You can do it.
- Today I will make progress towards my goals.
- My thoughts do not control me, I control my thoughts.
- I am capable of what I am willing to work for.
- I trust myself, and my instincts, above anyone else.
- To love myself, is the ultimate love.
- To make small steps towards big goals, is progress.
- There is no greater goal than being content with yourself.
- No one controls how I feel about myself, but me.
- To be positive is to be productive.
- No negative thought will take root in my mind.
- I am unique, so I will be uniquely successful.
- I believe in my ultimate potential.
- I do not need anyone's approval but my own.
- Never underestimate yourself. You are capable of great things.
- I am fulfilling my purpose in this world.
- I will achieve great things through small steps.
- If you are happy, you are motivated.
- I am thankful for what I have, even if it is not perfect.
- I will have a positive impact on someone else's day.
- My mind and my heart will remain open today.
- I can choose to make my curses, my blessings.
- My greatest struggles, are my greatest lessons.
- I will always remember that I only have control over myself, and my choices.

- I will learn what I do and do not have control of. I will let go of the latter.
- Always remember that you have enough, you do enough, and most importantly, you are enough.
- Be the person that you say you want to be. It is within your control.
- I am fierce. I am unafraid. I am bold.
- I will love myself the way that I say I want others to. They cannot do for me, what I will not do for myself.
- Create a life that makes you excited to get out of bed each day.
- Always choose kindness, you never know what someone is going through.
- Acts of kindness do not cost a thing, but they return to us great riches.
- If it does not serve you, sever it from your life.
- If I wish for it, I need to be willing to work for it.
- I believe in myself. I am capable of whatever I set my mind too.
- I can be kind, fierce, and brave – all at the same time.
- I do not need to put anyone down, to build myself up.
- I give myself permission to go after what I want.
- If it was easy, it would NOT be worth it.
- Never miss a chance to make someone's day. You never know when you changed their day.
- Never forget that you write your own story. So make it one you will never forget.
- Lessons and wisdom is all around us if we are only willing to listen.
- I already have everything I need.
- I will express my appreciation for those I love each day.
- I will not take for granted that people know what I love and appreciate about them.
- I release all the negativity within me, and open myself up to happiness and opportunity.

This is the end of the quotes. Hope you enjoyed it. We are now switching to a quick hypnosis session, so get ready and let's begin.

SELF-ESTEEM HYPNOSIS

You can do this hypnosis with your eyes closed for a much better experience.

Be prepared as we will begin the session of hypnosis to improve your self-esteem:

1. Before you begin rate your confidence on a scale of 1 – 10 (low to high.) Without this step, you won't know if the experiment worked -- or not.

2. Think about someone who loves and/or admires you. It could be a parent, a child, a friend, co –worker, acquaintance, or relative of any kind.

3. Imagine having a light, normal conversation with that person for a minute or two. This will help loosen your mind and start a flow. Start with a greeting and casual banter. What would you say? How would they reply?

4. As you are having this conversation, imagine that your consciousness rises up out of you and enters the person who loves and admires you, so that you can see through their eyes, hear through their ears and feel their feelings of openness, kindness, admiration and love.

5. Notice from this point of view, how "that you" looks. What do you look like through the eyes of love? What are the qualities, the characteristics that make that you special? What are your gifts?

6. Write down observations as if you were THAT person writing about your heartfelt love and admiration for THAT YOU.

7. Why does this person love and respect you? What do those feelings feel like? What do they see, hear and feel? If this person was writing about you, what else would they say?

8. Now allow your consciousness to be fully present in your own body and read your observations out loud.

9. How do you feel now? Rate yourself again on a 1- 10 scale.

This hypnosis session is over, let's jump to the next one.

HYPNOSIS FOR CONFIDENCE

Now let's boost your self-confidence by starting this hypnosis session. Get prepared, we are about to begin.

- First identify your challenge. Do you have something that you feel insecure about, that you want to boost your confidence about? This might be an important conversation with a spouse or family member or even your boss.
- It might be a speech you have to give or a task you have to do, it might be a sports performance or meeting new people. Whatever it is identify it now. As you come aware of your issue you can change it.
- If you do not identify it you cannot change it. So take the time to note what it is that might be holding you back from feeling capable and confident. What triggers it and where and when you first encountered this feeling, anything your parents or friends said to you, any believes you might hold because of these comments or experiences? Now this is what you want to change.
- Read through all of the following one or two times.
- Then take a deep and satisfying inhale, hold it for one moment and let the air slowly escape through your nose or mouth. Do this three times each time allowing yourself to relax and calm your body twice as deep with every exhale, letting your muscles become loose and limp like a loose rubber band.
- Take time to travel through all of your body from toes up to your head or from your head down into your toes, it doesn't matter where you start...you just relax...and it doesn't matter where you relax first... Say to yourself: Any time I do this again I will get better at it and I will relax quicker, easier and deeper.

- Now allow your mind to float back to an event that you can be proud of... where you indeed have accomplished something that at first seemed impossible or far out...we all have made experiences like this before.
- Then allow your mind to wander to such an event...counting backwards from 5 to 1 and at the count of 1 you will be there...instantly. 5 floating back, 4 feeling relaxed and comfortable floating, 3 almost there, 2 feels so good to just float, 1 be there!
- As you are there, now ...notice what you see, every color, every shape, people around you, where are you? What are you wearing, shoes, pants/ dress...what are you hearing? Any sounds, music, voices? what are people around you saying? What are you saying to yourself?
- Notice how you feel... and let that positive feeling flood your whole body... let it expand, melt into every cell, every muscle, every tissue. Breathe again and let the exhale take you even deeper...more intense, more vivid into that feeling!
- Now... let that positive emotion take you further back like floating back along an invisible timeline, magically drawn to the previous event before this event that is important for you to know ...floating effortlessly and easily into another event, notice how well you are doing and how that feels...let that emotion flood through your whole body again but this time ten times more intense and deeper, notice everything, soak it up like a sponge, you are right in it...
- Now let that feeling take you back one more time ...floating high up and back, magically drawn to another event in the past ... to another event an event where you felt good about yourself, pleased and even surprised at how well you did, take it all in again...what do you see, what do you hear, how do you feel?... you have surprised yourself many times in your life already, haven't you?
- You have achieved something already which you might have forgotten about or just did not focus on because we tend to focus much more on all those things we do not have, that we have lost or failed at. Now congratulate yourself for achieving

so much...

- Now gently float back towards the present, floating effortlessly just by yourself forward ... drifting to a time in the future taking all the new insight and learning with you, taking look at where you have indeed surprised yourself in the future ...in your own and delightful way... where you have succeeded in something that you previously believed you could not do... Something that might have been challenging before but now is leaving you calm and at ease...as you have taken with you what you needed and surprised yourself and others...
- Feel what it feels like in your body, see what you can see around you. People? Colours, furniture, nature, make it really vivid, intense and bright. Hear what you can hear as people might congratulate you, or comment in a positive way.
- You might even smell something pleasant and specific for you that is in connection with your success and feeling confident and good about yourself. You might be wearing a specific outfit...notice and intensify everything that is happening.
- You have a choice now, you can take a gift with you into the future:
- You can take a picture of your most intense experience of the successful event with you and keep it in your heart; where anytime you need to see it, it will be there for you to remember and you will remember everything instantly
- Or you can turn the deepest sensation of the event into a scent ,a perfume which anytime you smell it, it will instantly trigger your deep feelings of confidence again.
- Or you can give the deepest and most profound feeling of the successful events a name and any time you say the name in your mind you will feel it again, just as deep and profound in your whole body.
- You are already creating a new you... surprising yourself with new delightful ways of creating success and confidence... the new you...and any time you do this visualization/ self hypnosis again you will be better at it and you will go deeper, finding more achievements and successes in your life...you

will relax and feel better in every way each time you use this exercise, as it is the nature of human beings to get better with practice...and you can open your eyes as soon as your subconscious mind has absorbed all the new learning and saved it for all future events. As you open your eyes feeling refreshed and energized.

You can now relax; this session is over. Our next stop is a Self-Worth visualization session that is going to help you to reach a state of excellent self-worth.

SELF-WORTH VISUALIZATION SCRIPT

Having an excellent self-worth makes a person do spectacular things, and in this script we will be doing a visualization script that promotes self-worth.

- Induction of choice (Speak with empathy and be congruent)
- Everything we do will be so easy and relaxed...just simply relax even more now.
- Now, picture a tranquil lake...See how the sun glints off the water.
- See a bird gliding gently overhead...so tranquil and calm...you are tranquil and calm...And now, there is energy gathering in the sky above you. It is a gentle loving energy. It looks like little particles of silver and gold, little particles of light. The silver and gold specks gather above you and begin to swirl around, around and around. A gentle easy swirling. A gentle loving feeling...
- Now all this gentle loving energy is dipping down to you in a cone of energy...a swirling cone of loving energy, peaceful energy, and gentle energy. It dips down and covers your head, clearing your mind of any negative thoughts. It clears your mind of all criticism, all judgment.
- It clears your mind of any blocks you have in your way, any negative patterns of thinking. It clears your mind of all worry about the future, all regret for the past. It clears you of thoughts which make you uncomfortable or afraid. It clears the negative thoughts and replaces them with a deep, deep quiet...a wonderful peace and calm.
- Feel the calm and peace fill your mind. Now the cone of energy dips lower and covers your throat. And here, it clears away the things, which keep you from expressing yourself fully and openly and lovingly. It opens your throat so that you can speak your truth. Now the energy cone dips lower and covers your heart.

- And here it takes away the anger and the blame and replaces it with forgiveness. It takes away the longings and regrets, the jealousies and any feeling that there us something you are missing, any yearnings that make you think that happiness lies somewhere in the future.
- If only things were different in some way. Instead of this longing, this feeling of loneliness and emptiness, your heart, is now filled with love. The empty loneliness is cleared away and you are filled with the love of the universe in its place.
- Now the cone of energy dips lower and covers your stomach, your solar plexus. Here it takes away the fear and replaces it with a comfortable feeling, A deeply centered feeling that all is right with the world. A centered feeling that makes you feel as if you are exactly right, exactly what you need to be in this moment. Now the cone dips down and covers the rest of your body.
- And here you feel deeply rooted to this physical experience, very much part of the earth, very much part of all that is. All fear of this physical existence is swept away in the cone of energy.
- Now the cone expands and it spreads to cover the entire room in which you are sitting. It clears the room of all negative energy, of conversations and feelings which occurred here, recently and for years past. All that old negative energy is cleared and only positive energy remains...now the cone expands further and covers the entire [building] in which you are sitting. Again, it swirls around and around clearing away the negative leaving the positive.
- Now the energy lifts up slowly...slowly...lifts up and returns to the sky...swirling and taking with it all of the negative energy which was removed, and sends this to the light where it is accepted and transformed. And now you feel completely clean and clear. You feel as if you were just born, brand new and ready for life and love.
- See the angels that appear above you. They are dressed in long white gowns and they glow golden with love. They each have a gleaming silver pitcher full of love and they pour it

over you now. They pour their love on you. They pour their love on the room in which you are sitting and on every room in the building. They pour on love and love and love, more and more love.

- You feel it filling you, blessing you. You feel the sweet waters of love filling the places where the negative energy was swept away. It fills you completely, it fills you so full you begin to overflow and love spills out from you, the sweet waters of love, spilling out and reaching out to everyone in your life. Reaching out...touching everyone. See the waters flow...See the waters pour down...fill you and overflow and reach out to everyone in your life.
- Feel what it is like to be filled with love, feel what it is like to be loved, completely loved, absolutely loved, nothing but love. Experience this, revel in this. Laugh, smile, and open your mouth to drink in this love. Rub it all over your body. Laugh with joy at the wonder of it...all this love... poured down on you, an endless stream of love, and it is all for you. Where there was fear, there is now love, where there were negative thoughts, now there is love and positive thoughts. Where there was guilt, now there is love...love...washing clean? Love filling up. Love embracing you.
- You are exactly as you need to be. You have tried so hard and you have done well. You have not done everything you have hoped to do and that is all right. Exactly as you are you should be. What you have done has been good. What you have left undone is good as well. You are now exactly where you need to be in order to take the next step in your life, on your path. You are all that you need to be.
- There is nothing missing. There is nothing lacking. You are strong and capable and are exactly what you ought to be in all ways. Accept yourself; accept yourself exactly as you are. Have you made some mistakes? Of course you have. And those mistakes were exactly what you needed to lead you to this perfect moment, right now, exactly where you are...ready to take the next step in your life.

- Have you left things undone with regret? Let the regrets go...For everything you have done and left undone is exactly what has led you to now, this moment. This moment is exactly as it should be and so are you. Accept yourself, accept that you are worthy of the great love of the universe. See above you how the angels are gathering.
- Yes, there are the angels who are pouring love upon you, unending love, and there are angels behind them, row after row of angels, filling the sky with their glory and wonder. They are all sending their love and their blessing down upon you.
- And you, exactly as you are, are worthy of all this love. Yes, you are. You are worthy of it and surrounded by it. There is help for you at every turn because you are this worthy. You are everything. You are an important part of all that is. You are the piece that makes the puzzle whole. You are the note which makes the chord complete. You are vitally important. And healing yourself heals the world. Loving yourself fills the world with love. You are connected to all that is...
- Feel this deeply...Feel this in your core. Feel the deep connection which runs down into the earth and up to the heavens...Feel the deep connection which runs through you...Feel the oneness and feel how you are part of that oneness...
- How it could not exist without you. **YOU ARE THIS IMPORTANT.**
- **YOU ARE WORTHY OF LOVE AND YOU ARE WORTHY OF RESPECT.** Respect yourself deeply. Love yourself deeply. Treat yourself with deep respect. Treat your body with respect, giving it pure water and healthy food, exercising it and pampering it.
- Treat your mind with respect, providing it with times of peace and quiet in order to let it clear and recharge. Treat your emotional self with respect by demanding that others treat you well, by speaking up for yourself by making choices and decisions, which help you. Act in your own best interest,

- respect others, yes, **BUT NOT MORE THAN** you respect yourself.
- Love others, yes, but not more than you love yourself. Begin with yourself always. Begin here, within yourself, loving yourself, respecting you and then let that glow reach outward.
- See now...the spark inside you...see the glow inside you. This is the glow of your being, your creativity, your love of life and self. Now let it expand, let it fill you, this glow. Let it glow, grow, and fill your entire body until you are alight with whom you are. Shine, shine with who you are. All of your talents let them shine.
- All of your humor let it shine. All of your deepest beliefs, your personal truth, let it shine. All of your love, your love for life itself, let it shine. Now... let the glow reach out even further than you, let it glow brighter and brighter until you are a beacon of love and caring, able to light the way for others as well.
- This is your goal...to let yourself be seen in all of your beauty ...To let yourself glow so brightly that you light up this world. You can do this. In all the perfection of being, you can do this. Shine... shine...shine
- Now just sit quietly for a few moments and feel yourself shine, see yourself shine...shine...And now take a few deep breaths...That's right...Move your toes around, then your legs. Move your hands and then your arms. Lift your arms up over your head and stretch. Roll your shoulders gently. Take a deep breath and open your eyes...wide-awake...back to full conscious awareness.
- **NOW, AS YOU GO OUT IN THE WORLD TODAY, REMEMBER TO SHINE!**

WE ARE NOW SWITCHING TO A NEW LISTING OF SELF-ESTEEM AFFIRMATIONS, SO GET READY AND LET'S BEGIN.
SELF-ESTEEM AFFIRMATIONS
- Let's say that your goal is to be more social and spontaneous when you are with many people around. You can work similarly with other relative goals.

- When you finish your preparation, and you are in trance state then imagine that you walk down a circular stair. You barely see as there is low light. While descending, you relax even more, with every step.
- You finally reach a dark room. See the details of the room. You see some closed wooden doors from side to side. You know that something is going to happen when you open these doors, and so you feel somehow excited. You are going to be transformed and live some wonderful experiences; you know that, and that is why you feel like that. But first, you must change. You need something that will change you, something like a machine that will transform you.
- As you search the room for the machine, you see in the left corner a futuristic cabinet. This is the machine. You go in front of it, and you examine it. See its texture, its cables if any, if it is of glass or metal, imagine it as you like.
- You open the cabinet, and you go inside. It looks like a tanning pod and has a screen in front of you and a button. You step out of the machine, and you think again of your goal. What is this that you would like to change? Say it loud in the room, take a big breath and enter the machine again. You now see on the screen your goal. Take another big breath and while exhaling press the button and close your eyes.
- The machine now starts. You can imagine anything you want about its operation, like its sounds, lights, etc. For example, you can imagine that a penetrating yellow light hits you from every direction, and this makes you feel great.
- After a few seconds, the machine stops. Step out of it. You notice that you feel very relaxed and calm; you know you have changed, and you are excited to see your new ego in action.
- Go in front of a door that you saw when you entered the room. Take a deep breath, open this door and walk through it. You have now entered a new room while a party is taking place. There are a lot of people there, some familiar, some others completely strangers. You enter the room, and everybody notices your presence. You feel so relaxed and

comfortable, and your walk exhibits your high self-esteem aura.
- Everybody greets you, and you reply back in a very spontaneous manner. It looks like that this party has been set up for you. Everyone admires you. You are a very entertaining person attracting all the attention. It's such a great experience that makes you feel beautiful.
- In the self confidence script, you imagine yourself as you wanted to be. You are not afraid anything, and you have total trust in yourself. This mental experience offers plenty of room for experimentation. You can imagine anything behind the door; a party, a job interview, a presentation or any situation that makes you feel nervous and uncomfortable.
- You can also pass more than one doors in a single session, experiencing more situations at the same time. Though, it is better to be focused on a single situation every time, especially in the beginning.
- Finally, feel free to change anything from the above story. The usual pattern you can use is to have a starting point like the dark room you entered, a mechanism that will transform you and an experience that you will behave as you always wanted. The rest are just details, the more details, the more vivid the scripts and the more real will look for your mind. If you have trouble in visualization, then try first some visualization exercises.
- Remember to repeat this many times, keeping the same goal and one day you will realize that you act as you always wanted.

SELF-CONFIDENCE HYPNOSIS SCRIPT

Now get ready as we will be starting a new session of hypnosis to boost your self-confidence:

- From this moment on... you're feeling and you're becoming more and more confident... each and every day... and this wonderful suggestion... this wonderful idea... this wonderful belief of you becoming... and you feeling more and more confident each and everyday... is now growing strong inside your mind.... this wonderful, positive suggestion... this wonderful, positive idea... and this wonderful belief... that you're becoming... that you're feeling... more and more confident every single day... is becoming more and more real for you... each and everyday.... you're truly feeling more confident each and everyday...

- You're becoming more and more confident... and this is allowing you to do more things in your life.... as you become... and as you feel more and more confident... every single day... it's giving you a wonderful freedom in your life... a wonderful freedom to do new things... a wonderful freedom, just to be who you want to be... without those unnecessary feelings of anxiety or worry... the confidence to be who you want to be..

- A wonderful... strong... positive confidence... is growing strong in you now... so that you can do what you want to do in your life... in fact, from this moment on... it can feel for you, like a weight... it can feel like a burden has been lifted off your shoulders... because with every single day that passes by... every part of you feels more confident... with every single day that passes by... every single part of you is becoming more and more confident.... more confident in yourself... more confident about the world around you... more and more confident to do those things... that you've always wanted to do...

- The freedom... the complete freedom in your life... and your unconscious mind... takes this suggestion.... your unconscious mind takes this idea... of you being and you feeling more and more confident... every single day and your unconscious mind... makes this confidence in you stronger and stronger... more and more real for you...
- And as you now continue to relax more and more... with every breath... as you continue to drift deeper and deeper... into this wonderful relaxing state... each and every one of these suggestions... each and every one of these positive ideas... grow strong in your mind... become more and more real for you... not because I say so... but because these are the suggestions that you want in your life... and because these are the wonderful positive suggestions that you want in your life... each and every one of these suggestions grow stronger for you... each and every one of these suggestions become more and more real for you...
- And as you relax more with every breath... I would like you now to imagine... or to think, in your mind's eye... just whatever works best... imagine or think like you are stood in front of a full length mirror... and as you imagine being stood in front of a full length mirror... as you imagine looking at that reflection of yourself... you begin to notice a big difference... because as you look at that reflection...
- You're looking at somebody who truly feels extremely confident... you're looking at someone who's becoming and is feeling... more and more confident every single day... notice how that reflection is stood... they're stood tall... they're stood proud... and you can tell just by the look of the refection... that this is somebody who truly is extremely confident...
- This reflection has a wonderful freedom... a wonderful freedom in their lives' to do things... to go places... to be who they want to be... and as you imagine looking into the eyes of that reflection... that part of you who truly wants to feel and to be confident for some time... begins to wonder... begins to wonder what that reflection knows about being confident...

that you want to know... and it's something that you need to know...
- So just imagine now... or think in your mind's eye... like you were stepping into that reflection... was merging with that reflection... and as you merge with that reflection... and as you become one with that reflection... it does feel like a weight... it does feel like a burden has been lifted off your shoulders... and every part of you feels confident... every part of you is confident... every part of you now has a wonderful freedom... a wonderful freedom to be who you want to be..

This hypnosis session is now over. Let's start the next session.

SELF-CONFIDENCE HYPNOSIS

- Begin with a relaxation exercise to help you relax. You might try a fractional relaxation exercise. Start by breathing deeply for several breaths and then focus on relaxing the different parts of your body.
- Start by relaxing your scalp, your forehead, your eyes, your jaw, etc.
- Once you're relaxed, think about something you do well and allow yourself to feel good about that thing. It doesn't matter what it is; it could be a particular sport, math, making friends, selling something, great taste in clothes, compassion for others, art, cooking, and on and on. See yourself doing this thing and allow yourself to feel good about it.
- And go ahead and smile. And appreciate the fact that you're really good at this thing, and understand that not everyone is as good at this thing as you are. They might be good at some things, but maybe not as good as you are at this thing.
- And allow a feeling of confidence to begin to grow within you. And it's all right for you to feel some pride as well.
- And now think of something else that you do well. Something that you're better at than a lot of people. And allow your appreciation of yourself to grow and get bigger. Feel this appreciation growing inside you. And now think of a third thing, maybe it's kindness or thoughtfulness or charity.
- A personal trait that helps define who you are. And notice how this good feeling is now permeating your entire being. And allow yourself to enjoy that feeling for a while.
- After allowing yourself to feel good about yourself for a while, see yourself at some kind of social gathering. And bring those good feelings with you. Notice how natural it feels to feel good about yourself, to appreciate yourself, to feel relaxed and confident--because you understand that like everyone else at that social gathering, there are things that you excel at.
- And you don't feel any need to let others know about those things that you do well because it's enough that you know.

- You should repeat this exercise and continue to focus on the things that you do well for at least a month or two, until the positive thoughts about yourself begin to push aside and overwhelm the old, negative self-perception.

THIS SESSION IS OVER; WE WILL NOW KEEP GOING WITH THE NEXT SESSION.

SELF-ESTEEM HYPNOSIS

FOR OUR LAST SESSION WE WILL BE DOING SELF-ESTEEM HYPNOSIS. PREPARE YOURSELVES AS WE WILL BE STARTING THE SESSION, TO BEGIN:

- Find a warm, comfortable place where you can relax and not be disturbed for around fifteen minutes. This script is to be read slowly and deliberately
- Begin by trying to roll your eyes back up into forehead and keep them there. You will quickly begin to feel your eyes feeling heavy and tired. Hold your eyes in this position for as long as you can before they simply have to close.
- Now, with your eyes closed, take a deep breath in through your nose and out through your nose. Notice how the air feels cold as it hits your nostrils on inhalation and warm as you exhale. Build a rhythm of slow, deep breathing.
- Begin to visualize yourself in the third person, as if you are having an outer body experience. You look calm and perfectly relaxed. Your breathing is steady and your body is loose and limp. Focus entirely on yourself, in this visualization you are the only thing that matters. There is no background or any other objects to distract you. Just your own body in this peaceful state.
- You start to feel yourself moving down. Visually it is hard to tell that you are moving down, but you get that unmistakable feeling that your body is sinking ever downwards towards something that you cannot yet see. As your body is taken down you begin to feel a warmth in your stomach. This warmth spreads all throughout your body.
- It is now you realize that you are back in your own body, no longer looking on from afar. No sooner have you noticed that you are back inside your body but you also notice that the darkness around you has lifted and you are now laid back in a hammock that supports your body and sways gently in the warm breeze.

- As you look around you realize you are at a beach, but not just any beach. This is the most beautiful beach you could possibly imagine. The sea is a clear, crystal blue, the sand is a golden yellow and there is just a few white wispy clouds floating in the sky. The warmth of the sun radiates all over your body...you are the only person on your own personal dream beach.
- As you bask in the beauty all around you, it is time to repeat your positive affirmations to yourself – whatever they be.
  (Repeat your affirmations around twenty times. There is no need to count, just stop when you feel the time is right.)
- I would now like you to spend some type thinking about what actions you are going to take to achieve your goal. Positive thinking is important, but without taking action thoughts are just thoughts. To breath life into them you must take action. So think about what you are actually going to do to make your affirmations come true.
  (For the confidence example used above you could take acting classes, talk to people in situations that you normally wouldn't or thrust yourself into positions where you have to speak in public.)
- Now that you have set a goal and decided how you are going to achieve it, it is time to wake up. When you wake up you will remember everything you have thought during this session and feel motivated to turn these thoughts into action.

At the count of ten you will wake up fresh and alert and ready to achieve your goals.

1...Waking up.

2...

3...

4...Eyes beginning to flutter open.

5...

6...

7...Eyes open now.

8...

9...Aware of your surroundings.

10... Fully wide awake.

This book about Motivational Affirmations to Boost Confidence and Self-Esteem with The Most Powerful Subliminal Affirmations, Hypnosis and Quotes is now over.

I encourage you to listen to this book recording from time to time when you have spare time before you rest or directly after you woke up in the first part of the day or whenever you need to.
Set aside the opportunity to listen again to these affirmations and quotations as they will propel you and lift your spirit up.
Lastly, if you enjoyed this book I ask that you please take the time to review it on Amazon.com. Your honest feedback would be greatly appreciated.
Thank you.
Now, I would like to share with you a free sneak peek to another one of my books that I think you will really enjoy. The book is called "Emotional intelligence 2.0: A Practical Guide for Beginners" Published by Travis Goleman and Daniel Greaves. It's A Practical Guide that will teach you to master Social Intelligence, Emotional Awareness and Relationship Management. You will also learn How to use Conversational Skills to Persuade and Influence People.

Enjoy!

INTRODUCTION

You have heard so much about emotional intelligence that your interest is piqued. Whether you are a top-management official at work or a stay-at-home mom, emotional intelligence is important in your life. I commend you for taking the steps to develop your emotional intelligence skills. By doing so, you will only improve your quality of life from how you feel about yourself to how you feel about others, and ultimately, how others feel about you.

I can do all that just by reading this book, you may ask? Yup! You sure can.

The following chapters will discuss how you can develop your ability to master emotional intelligence and to see great improvements in your personal and professional life. The book is divided into 6 easy-to-read chapters that will give you insight into how to manage your emotional intelligence.

The first chapter will give a brief overview of what emotional intelligence is. Then the subsequent chapters will break down the tenets of emotional intelligence into more detail. Chapter 2 builds on Chapter 1 and explores what emotional intelligence looks like in your everyday life. From this chapter, we dive right into building skills that will help you improve your emotional intelligence. In Chapter 3, how to manage your emotions will be discussed, followed by how to improve your self-awareness in Chapter 4. Chapter 5 explains how to use social awareness and relationship management respectively.

At the end of every chapter, there will be a special section dedicated to giving you skills on how to develop each skill in order to become better at emotional intelligence. Also, please note that throughout the chapters, you will learn about Valerie who does not have an idea about emotional intelligence and her socially bankrupt life reflects it. Please do not be like Valerie!

Hopefully, by the end of this book, you will learn a lot from Valerie on what to do and what not to do in regards to emotional intelligence. At the end of the chapter, bullet points of the chapter topics and activities you can do to help develop your emotional intelligence will be given. Take small baby steps and do not be afraid to feel awkward as you try to implement the changes associated with emotional intelligence into your life. Every journey must start with one step and it is difficult before it gets easier. By the time you finish, you will notice how much your life has improved just because you decided to take the step to be more emotionally intelligent.

There are plenty of books on this subject on the market, so thanks again for choosing this one! Every effort was made to ensure it is full of as much useful information as possible. Please enjoy!

CHAPTER 1: WHAT IS EMOTIONAL INTELLIGENCE?

Meet Valerie. Valerie is a typical American who is married with two kids, a house, and a white picket fence. Oh yeah, she has a beautiful black Labrador as well. Valerie would consider her to have an average level of emotional intelligence. She does ok at work. Her familial, personal, and professional relationships are so-so. She feels like she's walking through life. Not going fast or slow, but just regular shmegular. She doesn't always feel in control and sometimes has panic attacks because she is overwhelmed, stressed, and unhealthy. She figures everyone else is going through the same things so it is not a big problem.

Cut to one busy day where Valerie is rushing to work because she has not communicated to her family members that she needs help and all of the chores and housework falls on her. Not too mention, she had to stay late at work the night before because she is a people pleaser which made her oversleep in the first place. Picture Valerie in a car, speeding down the highway in the rain before she hydroplanes smack dab into an eighteen-wheeler. Her car spins out of control and Valerie finds herself pinned behind her steering wheel in her car that is sideways in a ditch. Of course, a Good Samaritan saw the incident and immediately called emergency services who rushed to the scene. After the paramedics help her out the car, she is whisked to the hospital.

The good news is, she was alive. The bad news is, she has amnesia and she has to learn everything all over again. Facts like her children's names, her husband's name, and her dog's name will be seemingly easy to learn. However, the nuances of emotional intelligence seemed much more difficult to learn. She has to learn how to identify her personal emotions, manage them when reacting to other people, as well as managing her social settings and relationships. Whew! Valerie is on a quest to relearn what emotional intelligence is, but Valerie is not alone. There are a lot of people who want to learn how to be emotionally intelligent and are on the same path as Valerie.

This book attempts to help people like Valerie and the readers navigate the tricky, topsy-turvy, abstract world of emotions and the unspoken rules that come with it. Unlike Valerie who is starting with a blank slate, most people have some type of experience with their emotions whether they have anger issues, are people pleasers, or are narcissists. Emotional intelligence draws upon your personal preferences and experiences to figure out how to survive in the world. In order to improve upon one's emotional intelligence, one must first understand what emotional intelligence is.

So what is emotional intelligence? Known in short as EI, emotional intelligence is the multi-faceted capacity of being in tune with your personal thoughts and emotions and being able to manage them in your daily living and in your dealings with other people. In order to be emotionally intelligent, you must first have mastery of who you are and know how to handle your emotions. Then you must know how to navigate relationships with other people, especially how to interpret and understand their emotions and how to be savvy in the way you respond to their emotions for optimal results. In other words, to be emotionally intelligent, you need to know what to say, when to say it, and how to say it. Sounds like a lot? You're right. Becoming emotionally intelligent can be overwhelming, but it is not impossible. It is a skill that can be learned with practice. Being emotionally intelligent is a trait many want to acquire because research has shown that emotionally intelligent people are deemed better leaders, better friends, and better family members. People with emotional intelligence do not necessarily have the highest IQ, but they understand how people work. As a result, their acumen in dealing with people helps them to be successful in a way that people who are not emotionally intelligent are not able to achieve.

Emotional intelligence was brought to the mainstream in 1995 by Daniel Goleman when he wrote the book *Emotional Intelligence: Why It Can Matter More Than IQ*. This book was seminal in changing how people thought about the power of emotions. Before this book, emotions were not seen as powerful tools to help you succeed. Emotions were seen as a hindrance. Goldman brought the importance of being emotionally intelligent to the forefront, but it was not an idea that originated with him. Way back in the day, over 2,000 years ago, Plato wrote that "All learning has an emotional base." Even though Plato had said that emotions were important centuries earlier, scientists did not always see it that way. However, in the 1920s, the idea that emotions were important re-emerged when Edward Thorndike named the ability to get along with others as "social intelligence."

In 1950, Abraham Maslow sparked the human potential movement and wrote about the importance of people enhancing their mental, physical, emotional, and spiritual strengths. From his research, lots of similar movements were launched and people began to build on his ideas. From this birth of new knowledge, two researchers, Peter Salovey and John "Jack" Mayer in the 1990s, have been credited with first using the term 'emotional intelligence.' In the article, Salovey and Mayer defined emotional intelligence as scientifically testable "intelligence." This work set the foundation for Daniel Goleman's book in 1995. From there, many different offshoots of emotional intelligence were developed. For the purpose of this book, we will focus on emotional intelligence as being composed of four different parts consisting of self-management, self-awareness, social awareness, and relationship management.

Self-awareness is being in tune with your emotions. If you are self-aware, you are great at identifying and deciphering your emotions and using them effectively when you react to a situation. Self-management is the act of managing your emotions and the reactions to any situation you may find yourself in. The word 'manage' is key in the definition of self-management. If you are great at self-management, it does not mean that you do not get angry or experience emotions at all. It means that you are adept at how you manage those emotions to get the outcome you want. Social awareness is being keen to the social environment around you. And relationship management is all about handling your relationships whether they be professional, personal, or even the relationship with yourself. In later chapters, each separate component will be delved into in greater detail.

To understand how one learns about emotional intelligence, a person must understand how our brains work. Our brain is divided into three separate parts — the basal ganglia, limbic system, and neocortex. The basal ganglia are at the root of our brain and it is considered the place where all our instincts reside. When you feel something in your gut, the information travels directly to this region of your brain without going through the other regions. This is information that you do not have to think about at all. The next part of the brain is the limbic system. The information processed by this part of your brain is considered to be processed on the subconscious level. Subconscious level information is a step above unconscious information and that information is right below our level of awareness. The subconscious level is where our emotions reside. It stores information about experiences good and bad that affect our behaviors, as well as it stores our value judgments. The neocortex is the next part of the brain. It controls your level of awareness. The information in this part of the brain is able to be accessed at will. It controls our reasoning, language, and thoughts. This brief overview of the brain is helpful to understand because certain activities suggested later on in the book target certain aspects of the brain. It is a cool tidbit to understand how the activities strengthen certain aspects of your brain so you can learn how to control your emotional intelligence better and be more aware.

EMOTIONALLY INTELLIGENT CHARACTER TRAITS

How does someone who is emotionally intelligent act? People who are emotionally intelligent normally have a few characteristics that let others know they are emotionally intelligent individuals.

- Emotionally intelligent people have empathy. They are able to understand how others are feeling in any given situation. In other words, like the cliché says, emotionally intelligent people are able to walk in someone else's shoes. They are able to understand how someone with a sick child may be having a

rough time or understand the importance of being nice to everyone whether they have experienced that situation or not.
- Emotional intelligent people also think deeply about their emotions and other people's emotions – a lot. They are pros at knowing how to relate and manipulate to other people in order to get the best outcome possible.
- Emotionally intelligent people do not run from criticism. They are able to take feedback easily without being defensive. They are able to take what people say about them, dissect the criticism, and take from the criticism what they may.
- Emotionally intelligent people are also genuine people. They seek authenticity in their relationships with other people and tend to see the best in people. Hence, they also are able to forgive and forget slights against them rather easily.
- People who are emotionally intelligent are very positive. They are not angels. However, they are effective at refocusing their thoughts, so they do not act impulsively and do something that they will regret later.
- Emotionally intelligent people do not run from confrontation. They face the criticism head-on and then go from there. They handle the conflict with ease, even if their egos are wounded in the process.
- Emotionally intelligent people are excellent communicators. They know their personality type and communication style and are able to effectively communicate with others and know the style in which they prefer to be communicated.

People who are not emotionally intelligent tend to be the exact opposite.

- They are easily flustered and easily angered.
- They are selfish and they only care about one person - themselves.
- They do not think before they speak and they talk all the time without any care to how other people may react to what they are saying.
- People who are not emotionally intelligent are usually not the easiest people to get along with.

Emotionally intelligent people are leagues ahead of people who are not emotionally intelligent. Interestingly, one can have characteristics of being emotionally intelligent and also have characteristics of not being emotionally intelligent. The key is to try and work on your emotional intelligence until you are competent in all four areas of being emotionally intelligent. This takes work.

For someone who has never ever thought about learning more about emotional intelligence, the information explained thus far may seem suspect. You may be one of the people who believe that emotional intelligence is a fluke. You may think that it is not necessary or important to be in tune with your emotions or in tune with the emotions of others in order to be a better person. You may think emotional intelligence is nothing but hippy-dippy foolery that has no place in the same sentence with rational thought. You may think that emotional intelligence has no effect on your success. However, think of that one person that you would not rather be around. This person always makes inappropriate jokes. They never know what to say. It is like they always have a foot in their mouth. These types of people have no self-awareness. No one wants to be around them. This is why emotional intelligence matters. There is no black-and-white version of emotional intelligence.

It is possible that you are good with some of the aspects of emotional intelligence and you need help controlling the other aspects. Perhaps you are good at knowing your feelings and you're able to manage your emotions, but you are terrible at communicating with others. Hence, your relationship management needs work. Perhaps you are excellent at navigating relations and social settings, whether they are professional or personal because you are great at putting on a front but your personal life is in shambles. You may need to work on your self-awareness. Or perhaps, you can easily be wonderful at managing other people's relationships. You can be the one friend that everyone comes to when they need help, but you are horrible at your own self-management. It happens. Just because you are okay with three out of the four aspects of emotional intelligence does not mean that you cannot improve the other aspects. Wanting to be aware of how emotional intelligence works is commendable and there are definitely skills and exercises that you can do to improve each and every aspect of your emotional intelligence core.

Yet, emotional intelligence can have a dark side. There are some people who are master manipulators. They are so good at emotional intelligence that they can draw upon what someone else is feeling in order to get the outcome that they want. These people know how to pit people against each other, play the victim, and play on people's emotions to remain in control at all times. If you are not emotionally intelligent, you can really fall victim to their traps rather quickly. One of the most important reasons for developing your emotional intelligence is to be a better person and to protect yourself against people who have nefarious intentions.

Lucky for Valerie, she is starting with a blank slate when learning how to develop her emotional intelligence. She does not have to be concerned about all the baggage that comes with learning a new skill. For her, she has to begin by learning what emotional intelligence is. So buckle up. The next chapter will go into more detail about how emotional intelligence affects our daily life whether we are aware of it or not.

Chapter Highlights

- Emotional intelligence was coined by Daniel Goleman in 1995 by his book *Emotional Intelligence: Why It Is More Important Than Your IQ*.
- Emotional Intelligence is composed of four different parts — self-management, self-awareness, social awareness, and relationship management.
- Our brain is composed of three regions that control our thoughts and emotions. By doing exercises to improve every aspect of our brain, one can improve their emotional intelligence.

Do the Work

- Why are you interested in learning more about emotional intelligence? Is it to improve personally or is it to improve in a professional setting or is it another reason? Knowing why

- you want to learn about emotional intelligence can help you when you get to a difficult spot in your learning.
- Do you think that you have more traits of being emotionally intelligent or more traits of not being emotionally intelligent?
- Emotional intelligence is composed of four different components — self-awareness, self-management, social awareness, and relationship management. Which component do you think you need to work on?
- Before emotional intelligence was brought to the forefront, there was a philosopher who said that "emotions are at the base of every decision?" Who was it?

Thank you, this preview is now over.

I hope you enjoyed this preview of my book Emotional intelligence 2.0: A Practical Guide for Beginners by Travis Goleman and Daniel Greaves.

Please make sure to check out the full book on Amazon.com

Thank you.

www.ingramcontent.com/pod-product-compliance
Lightning Source LLC
Chambersburg PA
CBHW030112100526
44591CB00009B/378